Growing Classic Orchids

Growing Classic Orchids

AN ILLUSTRATED IDENTIFIER AND GUIDE TO CULTIVATION

Mike Tibbs
Ray Bilton

Sterling Publishing Co., Inc.
New York

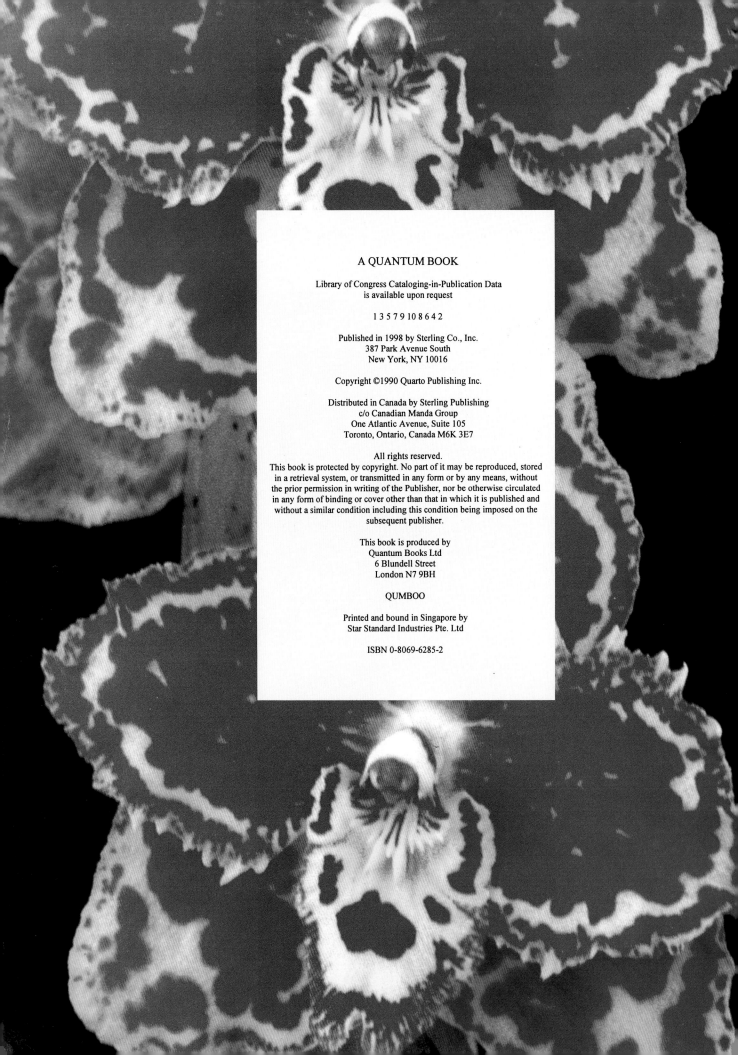

A QUANTUM BOOK

Library of Congress Cataloging-in-Publication Data
is available upon request

1 3 5 7 9 10 8 6 4 2

Published in 1998 by Sterling Co., Inc.
387 Park Avenue South
New York, NY 10016

Copyright ©1990 Quarto Publishing Inc.

Distributed in Canada by Sterling Publishing
c/o Canadian Manda Group
One Atlantic Avenue, Suite 105
Toronto, Ontario, Canada M6K 3E7

This book is produced by
Quantum Books Ltd
6 Blundell Street
London N7 9BH

QUMBOO

Printed and bound in Singapore by
Star Standard Industries Pte. Ltd

ISBN 0-8069-6285-2

CONTENTS

AUTHORS' NOTE

While this book in no way attempts to be a definitive work on orchids, we have tried to break down some of the fallacies associated with their cultivation. This has been set out in a simple fashion, so that the reader will know what type of environment and climatic conditions need to be provided for specific genera. The cultural information is original, having been drawn from the vast experience of the authors and the practical knowledge gained in the process of producing millions of orchid plants over a considerable number of years, and from their travels to the orchid centres of the world.

In these times, when we are becoming increasingly concerned about the future of our planet and its fauna and flora, we must ensure that we do not grow just any jungle – collected species. By selecting nursery-raised species and stock from legitimate commercial outlets which constantly strive to produce healthy plants and truly exciting hybrids, greater satisfaction will be achieved, as these plants will be substantially more vigorous than any jungle-collected plants.

LEFT: Miltonia Many Waters 'Robin'.

RIGHT: Masdevallia Veitchiana – the striking colour attracts many collectors

INTRODUCTION

O rchids are the most exciting of the flowering plants. They have always been considered difficult to grow, and once their cultivation has been mastered it could be said that the grower had graduated in horticultural terms. In this book the cultural methods have been simplified so that the reader can easily determine the environment needed for the various types of orchids.

Certainly they are the most fascinating, beautiful and sometimes bizarre plants, often showy with large brightly coloured flowers, yet on occasion almost microscopic in size. In fact, when looking at a diverse range of orchids in flower – with all the differences in size, shape, colour, scent or lack of it – it is sometimes difficult to believe that they all belong to the plant family known as *Orchidacae*.

The lifestyle that most people seem to lead today needs at least some time for relaxation, and there is no better therapy at the end of a stressful day than to step into the tranquil oasis of the orchid house where you will soon be entranced by the beauty of the flowers, the way a plant is rooting, or the strong new growth that is developing that gives confidence that the

FACING PAGE: Anselia Africano – *the bulb of this species has traditionally been chewed and sucked to remedy a range of illnesses.*

BELOW LEFT: Aerangis luteo alba *var.* Rhodesticta *and (below right)* Mystacidium venosum, *two African species.*

plant will produce fine flowers. Growing orchids is a deeply satisfying and therapeutic activity. Once you have embarked on the cultivation of orchids you will find that they are not like any other plant which may be only a passing phase; with these plants it can be a lifetime pursuit which gives great satisfaction both to yourself and those around you.

There are many persistent and commonly held beliefs about orchids – that they are parasites living off other plants; that they are difficult to grow; that they only flower every seven years; and that they all come from hot and steamy tropical jungles. The idea that orchids grow parasitically on other plants is false. They merely attach their roots around the branches of trees to gain support.

Again, are orchids really difficult to grow? Given the right climatic and cultural conditions they will, in fact, thrive anywhere. They will also flower regularly. Some orchids, such as the Phalaenopsis, may flower two or three times a year, and there is no reason why Cymbidiums should not flower annually. Nor do all orchids have to be grown in hot greenhouses. Nowadays many thrive quite happily as house-plants in a room or on a window-sill.

Most popular orchids will last longer in flower in the home than flowering azaleas or chrysanthemums and will give a lot more pleasure than continual bunches of cut flowers. The modern hybrids have evolved from almost 90 years of breeding, and will in many cases grow well in the home and certainly thrive in the greenhouse, shade house or conservatory. Nursery-raised stock acclimatizes much more readily after being moved into the home than do species uprooted from the tropical forests. Plants collected in the wild take months and sometimes years to begin to grow, if they survive at all.

Once the cultural needs of these fascinating plants are understood, growing them is relatively simple. Some orchids, for instance, come from high altitudes, where cool, damp and cloudy conditions prevail. In complete contrast, there are also tropical orchids which experience fairly long dry periods in their natural habitats. The truth is that orchids occur naturally in almost every geographical region of the world, except the arid deserts and permanent snowcaps.

THE NAMING OF ORCHIDS

The naming of orchids follows strict conventions, originally laid down by the Royal Horticultural Society in a publication called Orchid Registration and Nomenclature.

The terms used include:

Genus – *the family name; eg Paphiopedilum.*

Species – *a naturally occurring form of the genus; eg callosum.*

Hybrid – *offspring derived from the cross-pollination of two orchids. This name must be registered with the RHS; eg Maudiae.*

Parentage – *the maternal or pod parent and the paternal or pollen parent; eg P. callosum × P. lawrenceanum.*

Cultivar or varietal name – *an epithet used to distinguish a meritorious clone; eg 'Magnificum'.*

Award – *any distinction granted; eg FCC/RHS.*

The full title of the above plant will therefore be written as: Paphiopedilum Maudiae *'Magnificum'* FCC/RHS (P. callosum × P. lawrenceanum).

LEFT: Bulbophyllum lobbii 'Noddy', an orchid which attracts pollinators by the movement of its labellum.

ABOVE: Cymbidium forestii in Japan.

ABOVE LEFT: *A closeup of* Cymbidium forestii, *showing the flower.*

ABOVE RIGHT: Cymbidium viriscens *is seen here as a pot plant; this species has long been prized particularly by Japanese collectors.*

Orchids in cultivation

It is essentially for their eye-catching flowers that orchids are grown commercially today. There is, however, one orchid, the Vanilla orchid (*Vanilla planifolia*), which has economic value as the source of the familiar flavour used in ice-cream and cake recipes around the world. There are also a number of orchids which have been used by primitive peoples since time immemorial for medicinal purposes. The bulb of an African Ansellia species, for example, has traditionally been chewed and sucked as a remedy for various ailments.

A certain mystique has surrounded orchids for centuries. It can be seen in numerous old prints depicting oriental orchids, particularly in China and Japan. Orchids were admired by the Japanese at least as long ago as the eighth century. They were popular with the rising wealthy merchant class, while the less common varieties were particularly prized by court nobles. These species were selected for their rarity and their variety of colour, and they often cost hundreds of thousands of yen. The first orchid to be recorded in both written and graphic form by the Chinese was *Cymbidium ensifolium*.

In the past it was only rich land-owners who cultivated orchids, because they had the facilities to keep the plants warm enough during the winter. Today a much broader cross-section of people collect orchids as they become increasingly affordable. Prize orchids, selected breeding plants and rare specimens are, however, still expensive even today. But thanks to the modern propagation technique of tissue culture (see page 48), the price of orchids has fallen considerably.

The Orchid Register

The plant family *Orchidaceae* is the largest of all groups of flowering plants and contains at least 25,000 different species. This figure may, in fact, be much higher if all the variations within each group are taken into account. Hybridization has added considerably to the number of plants in cultivation since its first use more than a century ago. It was in 1853 that John Dominy, a Scottish gardener employed by an Exeter surgeon named John Harris, successfully crossed *Calanthe masuca* with *Calanthe furcata*. The resulting hybrid, named *Calanthe Dominyi*, subsequently flowered three years later.

A comprehensive register of all new orchid hybrids, known for many years as *Sander's Orchid Hybrid Lists* in honour of the St Albans grower who began it, is now run by the Royal Horticultural Society in London. There are now more than 75,000 registered hybrids, dating back more than a century. The register, which goes back to these early days, is available in book form. It has also been computerized and earlier errors have been corrected, so that it is now possible to obtain a print-out of the total register with few, if any, mistakes. The Orchid Register is unique in that it is the only plant register that lists the pedigrees through the hybrids' (grex) names. All the others use only varietal (cultivar) names.

Monopodial growth habit

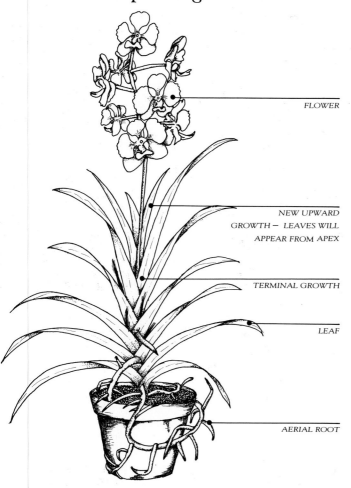

FLOWER

NEW UPWARD
GROWTH – LEAVES WILL
APPEAR FROM APEX

TERMINAL GROWTH

LEAF

AERIAL ROOT

The classification of orchids by growth habit

Orchids are generally divided into three main categories according to their different growth habits: epiphytes, lithophytes and terrestrials.

E P I P H Y T E S have adapted to the tropical jungle by clinging to tree branches in order to obtain light and air. Their name is taken from *epi*, meaning above or on, and *phyte* meaning plant. No orchid is parasitic: they simply grow on tree branches, often where a little humus has collected. Epiphytes often have specialized aerial roots which have a white spongy layer of cells called velamen. This protects the inner root tissues and absorbs water. These roots will also often dangle freely in the atmosphere.

L I T H O P H Y T E S are also found mostly in the tropics. They can be seen covering the bases and forks of trees or filling crevices in rocks. Here they can absorb a maximum supply of nutrients from decaying mosses, humus and washed-down soil. Some lithophytic orchids often have to endure prolonged dry periods. In these conditions they survive through their use of storage organs such as pseudo-bulbs and fleshy leaves.

T E R R E S T R I A L S occur in a range of climatic regions from cool temperate zones to the warmer tropics. These are soil-loving plants growing in the ground; most have a symbiotic relationship with a special fungus; this relationship is called *mycorrhiza*. This fungus invades the cells of the roots' outer layer, providing the plant with nutrients, and is essential for the seed germination of most orchids, particularly the European and North American terrestrial orchids. It is the lack of this fungus that prevents many terrestrial orchids from surviving when removed from their natural environment to an alien one. Even with today's technology, no substitute for *mycorrhiza* has yet been discovered. Much work has been done in recent years to isolate and culture it in laboratories so that this somewhat neglected group of orchids can become more available to the general public. This will also support the efforts of conservationists desperately battling to prevent the loss of these ever-decreasing orchids through needless destruction in their natural habitats. If, one day, we could wander through meadows overflowing in the spring with terrestrial orchids like carpets of bluebells or fields of poppies, that would be real progress.

BELOW: *Jungle collected orchids*

LEFT AND ABOVE: *Jungle collected orchids at a nursery in the Philippines.*

BELOW: *Recently collected specimens of* Angraecum philippinensis.

Conservation and protection

Charles Darwin once noted that a capsule of orchid seed, if germinated with the correct fungus, could produce a whole field of orchids. These, he added, could then produce enough further progeny to almost cover the British Isles and, in the next generation, the whole world. But, as he pointed out, the fact that we are not exactly wading through carpets of orchids shows that in nature orchid production is very much a matter of luck and natural selection. Only a few seeds in a million ever produce plants that reach maturity.

Collecting wild orchid plants in the tropical forests has long been a regular means of supply for orchid growers in many countries. Orchid-picking has been a traditional occupation for whole families for generations in the countries of origin. In the early days of collecting, around the turn of the century, it is known that many thousands of plants were lost when the ships carrying them went down at sea.

The conservation and protection of existing orchid stocks throughout the world has become a matter of prime importance. Hybridization has lessened to some extent the intense harvesting of plants in the tropical forests, but, as in any trade, there are always mercenaries who constantly over-

pick. Orchid habitats are certainly being destroyed in some parts of the world through deforestation. This is a result of the radical development policies being pursued in those areas and the activities of the indigenous peoples, who simply continue their ancestors' traditional practice of cutting down trees for fuel. Hopefully, the damage can be reduced in many areas by the introduction of education programmes and international grants.

It is obvious that, in areas of deforestation, it would be better to have the orchid species that are under threat of destruction salvaged. The plants could be made available initially to commercial institutions, which could multiply them either by raising seedlings or, in the case of selected clones, by using the modern technique of tissue culture (see page 48). This would, in turn, enable hobbyists with less experience to acquire these sought-after species. Some countries are already working on a programme of this kind by licensing legitimate orchid traders and hybridizers who are willing to follow procedures laid down by government bodies to monitor their activities. In other countries, however, restrictions are so tight that their trade is to some extent being hindered and limited.

Sympodial growth habit

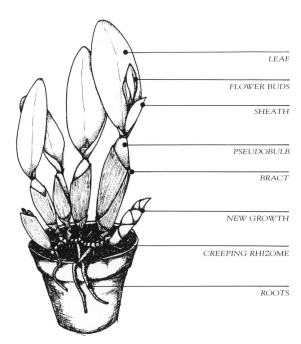

LEAF

FLOWER BUDS

SHEATH

PSEUDOBULB

BRACT

NEW GROWTH

CREEPING RHIZOME

ROOTS

LEFT: *Dendrobium hybrids ready for the auctions.*

RIGHT: *Cattleya flowers being packed for the auctions.*

BELOW: *Cattleya cut flower nursery.*

BOTTOM: *Nagoya Orchid Auctions*

FACING PAGE: *Orchid picking on Mindanao Island in the Philippines.*

International bodies and the orchid trade

The Convention on International Trade in Endangered Species of Wild Fauna and Flora (CITES) came into being in 1975. This body agreed to monitor the trade in orchid species around the world. This was done by implementing a permit scheme governing the import and export of plants. Some 80 nations joined the scheme and set up departments to deal with the new regulations. Each country, however, interpreted the regulations differently. This led some to create various loopholes, and others to put up obstacles.

CITES has unfortunately proved detrimental to the introduction of new species to leading commercial hybridists in some countries. As a result, the rarer species are not being multiplied. This is particularly true of new Paphiopedilum species discovered in China. Some botanists and conservationists claim that these have been almost totally cleared from the forests where they grow. Yet the hybridists who could and would multiply these plants have frequently been refused import permits.

In 1990 CITES issued new regulations governing trade in Paphiopedilum species. It had earlier declared that these were becoming extremely rare and that many of the 80 or so species were endangered, even though some botanists disputed this. Shortly before the new regulations came into force, orchid nurseries claiming to be traders in forest-collected plants bought up to three times their normal annual purchases of Paphiopedilum species in order to beat the deadline and to be able to continue trading in the ill-fated plants afterwards. This has created a nightmare for botanists. It has also been a blow to conservationists, as the collectors, their traditional livelihoods threatened, no doubt gathered the plants indiscriminately, even to the point of extinction.

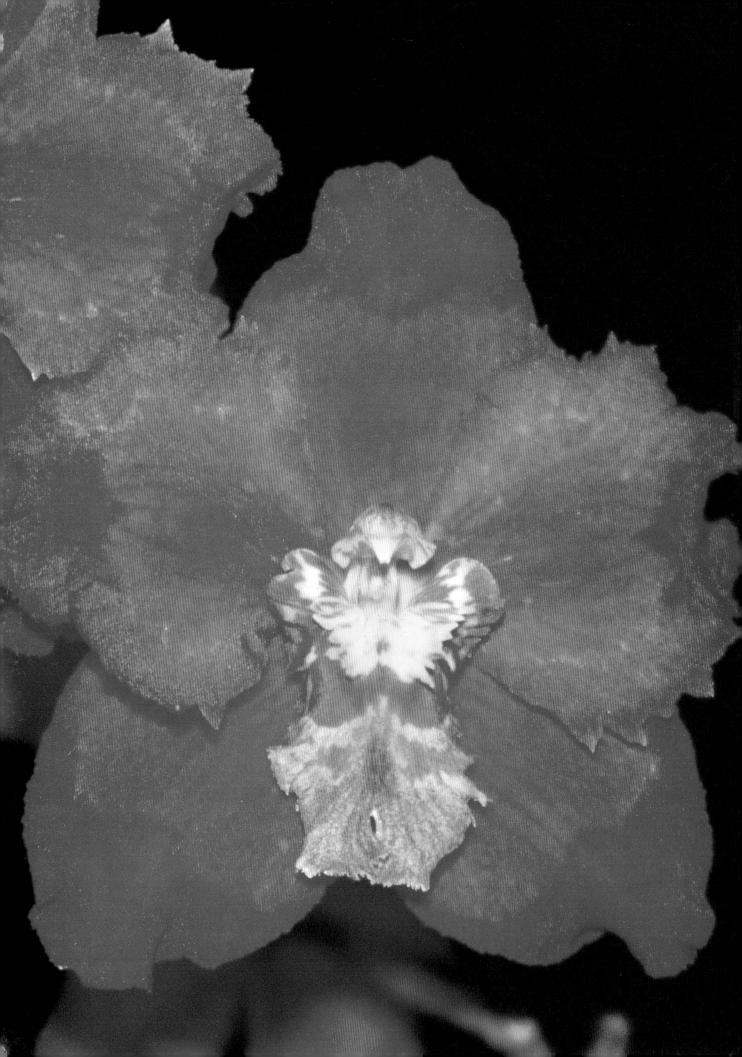

GENERAL CULTIVATION

The conditions in which you intend to grow your orchids must, of course, be suitable for them. However, many situations that were once considered impossible for orchid growing are now no longer thought to be so, but to succeed you must follow a little practical advice. First of all, always determine what conditions you will be able to offer your plants before making a final choice and going out to buy them. Remember, too, what conditions they need. Most cool-growing orchids, for example, come from the world's mountainous regions, which are often shrouded in mist and clouds. So they clearly will not thrive in hot, tropical conditions. The plants will not thrive and their flowers will wilt and fall within days if you try to grow them in such conditions.

Despite this, collectors constantly set themselves a challenge by trying to cultivate cool-growing species in warm, tropical climates, using various kinds of structures to provide the right conditions. In the same way, hobbyists in cooler climates regularly try their luck with the tropical orchids, often with great success.

FACING PAGE: Odontioda Ingmar 'Lyoth Glory'. *Odontoglossums are found predominantly in the mountainous regions of the Andes.*

RIGHT: Satyrium princeps, *an African terrestrial.*

Structures for orchid growing

Depending on the local climate, orchid growers around the world have devised various kinds of structures and shelters to provide their plants with suitable growing conditions. In areas where they are necessary, a choice of heating systems have also become available. When using these, however, you should avoid any that are likely to produce fumes, gases or gaseous odours harmful to plant life. Care should also be taken, and warnings heeded, when using gas-fired heaters. These should be checked and maintained regularly.

LEFT: *A weather station on a commercial glasshouse.*

RIGHT: *A modern glasshouse.*

SHADE HOUSES: in warmer climates, where glasshouses are not essential and favourable growing conditions exist, shade houses are quite adequate. These are constructed from wooden or iron poles covered with wire netting and shade-cloth. Roof coverings are also useful for those growers who wish to monitor more accurately the watering and feeding programmes of their plants.

LATH HOUSES are similar in construction to shade houses, but have coverings of evenly spaced wooden slats. These create successful growing conditions in tropical and sub-tropical climates.

CONSERVATORIES are becoming very popular in cooler climates for use as an additional room or a porch in which a tropical paradise can easily be created. They tend, however, to be expensive.

GLASSHOUSES may also be expensive, but they provide a controlled environment through the use of various manual, automatic and electronic devices to maintain the required growing conditions. Materials other than glass can be used in construction, such as fibreglass and polycarbonate materials. Although these materials are particularly expensive, they do not have the same devastating effect as broken glass.

POLYTHENE TUNNELS are occasionally used with good results to create greenhouse conditions without the high expense of glass and a rigid structure. The only drawback is that the plastic covering will last only for a certain period of time, depending on the sun's intensity. Polythene tunnels will not withstand adverse weather conditions and need to be sited in protected positions.

ENCLOSED SWIMMING POOLS, in sun lounges, conservatories or similar structures, tend to create a warm and humid environment which is ideal for growing tropical plants, provided there are no excessive amounts of chlorine gas.

European terrestrial orchids

In nature, terrestrial orchids occur in open forests, in meadows and on the banks of streams, where humus, decaying leaves and boggy areas exist. They often have tubers, which grow just below the surface of the ground. In general, terrestrial orchids are not ideally suited to pot culture, as any failure to meet their growing requirements often leads to fungal and bacterial rotting at the base. Some of the European terrestrials, especially Orchis, Ophrys and Dactylorhiza, are, however,

GREENHOUSES

There is an extensive range of greenhouses available today. While one must take into account the technical merit and scientific advantages that some offer, these features are not always necessary.

Most modern greenhouses are constructed using wooden or aluminium alloy frames. Timber-framed houses experience less heat loss than aluminium ones. The best wood is the Western Red cedar from North America, which is rot-resistant. If properly treated with protective water repellants every few years, these cedar houses can last a lifetime. A cheaper wood, but one which requires more regular maintenance, is the treated softwood Baltic pine. Aluminium alloy houses are generally maintenance-free. The framework is strong and fairly light; clips, rather than putty and nails, are used to hold the glazing in place. Glazing media include plastic, glass or polycarbonate sheets, with plastic giving the least insulation.

The cheapest and most easily constructed form of greenhouse can be made using a tubular frame covered with plastic sheeting. No foundation is necessary and the edges of the sheeting are buried in the ground. Ventilation is achieved by having a flap which opens at each end of the house.

Shading for the greenhouse may be achieved in various ways. A cool glass wash in white or green may be applied to the glazing. This is an efficient method of reducing the light levels and some products are easily removed by brushing with a soft broom. If this type of shading is used on a house where rainwater is collected in a butt, the water should not be used too soon after the application, as the pH of the collected water will be significantly affected. A more sophisticated form of shading is shade-cloth – a material made of woven plastic strands, available in varying weaves and thicknesses, giving different percentages of light exclusion. The latest variation of shade-cloth incorporates strips of aluminium foil woven into the cloth which also provides thermal insulation. In larger or commercial houses, the cloth may be made into horizontal curtains which run along tracks, giving a variable combination of light and insulation to prevent heat loss.

A layer of polythene sheeting inside the greenhouse offers added insulation by sandwiching a layer of air between it and the glazing. Bubble-plastic used the same way is even more effective, but dramatically reduces the light levels. Vents should not be covered in such a manner that they cannot open and close.

When planning the site for a greenhouse, the following points should be taken into consideration:

- **Level sites are preferable**. Foundations are easier and less expensive to lay.
- **The site should be well drained**. Stagnant water in the greenhouse will encourage fungal and bacterial disease.
- **An open position, away from large trees, is best.** Tall trees will not only obstruct the light, but in autumn, the leaves will block gutters, foul the glass and also harbour pests which may attack the orchids. Also damage could be caused by falling branches.
- **Exposure**. If possible, avoid a site which is overly exposed to strong winds, as this will increase the cost of heating the greenhouse.
- **Proximity to services**. Consider the distance for gas, electricity and water connections; also access during wet weather.
- **Aspect**. Ideally, the length of the house should run east-west. However, this is not always possible, and is not a prerequisite. In the Northern hemisphere, lean-to constructions against a south-facing wall will receive the most sun. North-facing houses are cooler and receive less light, but are still quite capable of growing fine plants. The converse obviously applies in the Southern hemisphere.

LEFT: *A simple shade house construction.*

RIGHT: *Computer systems in commercial nurseries are used to monitor climatic conditions, ventilation, shading etc.*

being grown successfully. Much work is also being done by various institutions, including Kew Gardens in London, to reintroduce many species back into nature from laboratory-raised stock.

In nature, the tuber produces a rosette of leaves and many new roots in the autumn after the summer dormancy period. These will mature over the winter and produce their inflorescences in the spring. Orchis, Ophrys and Dactylorhiza can be cultivated successfully in a cool alpine house and brought to flower either earlier or later than in nature by using controlled conditions.

The best time to select the plants is the dormancy period, when the leaves have dried and potting should be carried out. Terrestrials respond well to being repotted annually, as they cannot under any circumstances tolerate sour or decaying compost. Almost all composts are acceptable, but some species dislike too much peat. A good mix should include high-quality sieved garden soil, grit or sharp sand, and rich leaf mould. Although many terrestrials grow naturally in heavy clay and boggy composts, it is inadvisable to try to emulate these conditions in pot culture, as stagnant water will increase the risk of basal rot and other diseases. Animal manures and composts which might contain harmful pathogens should also be avoided.

After repotting, the plants may be placed outdoors. They should be returned to the cool alpine house, however, before there is any risk of frost, as this will blemish the foliage. The compost should be kept moist during the winter and the plants placed in fairly shaded positions. From mid to late spring, when the weather has become warmer, the plants may be put outdoors again.

Feeding is not advised if the plants are repotted every year. However, very weak concentrations of balanced fertilizer may be given during the growing period.

PLEIONES. Although Pleiones fall into the terrestrial category, they occur in nature in various habitats. They are relatively easy to grow, and require a cold rest period in the winter after losing their leaves and roots toward late autumn. Repotting should be carried out toward the end of the rest period in early winter. A compost containing bark, peat and perlite in equal quantities is desirable for these miniature gems. Extra crocks to ensure good drainage and fairly small pots are essential.

The compost must kept just damp until the flowers begin to show in early spring. The plants should then be watered carefully until the flowers fade. At this time a liquid feed at half the recommended strength should be given at alternate waterings. Through the summer months the plants should be given a semi-shaded position and good ventilation in order to keep temperatures below 85°F (29°C). Before late summer a potash-based fertilizer must be given to ripen the bulbs before the leaves fall and the plants enter their dormant period again.

ABOVE: Habenaria rhodesticta.

LEFT: Pleione formosana.

BELOW: Dactylorhiza foliosa, *an alpine house orchid.*

DISAS. Disas are cool-growing orchids that occur naturally on very damp river banks and in marshlands which are rich in humus. They enjoy the same climatic conditions as Odontoglossums, with a temperature range between 50 and 75°F (10–24°C). Temperatures outside this range can be harmful, except in midsummer, when slightly higher temperatures will be tolerated if the plants are in some shading and high humidity.

Disas have been grown successfully in various ways using hydroponic or hydroculture techniques, normal loamy composts and even live sphagnum moss. The main requirement is that the compost must retain some moisture and be free-draining. The plants must never be allowed to dry out completely and must be watered only with rain water. Highly chlorinated water and strong feeds are not advisable.

Repotting must be done in the autumn after the plants begin to die back and new shoots have begun to appear. The

ABOVE LEFT: Habenaria radiata.

ABOVE RIGHT: Disa chrysossachya, *a moisture-loving orchid.*

RIGHT: Habenaria tysonii.

BELOW LEFT: Disa Foam.

BELOW RIGHT: Epipactis gigantia

THE GROWING MEDIUM

Cymbidiums are ideally potted up in spring in a fairly open compost. All growers have their own favourite potting formula, but a mix of peat, perlite and bark is recommended for use in controlled greenhouse conditions. This compost will retain some moisture, but with adequate ventilation it should dry within a week in summer and possibly two weeks in late autumn and winter.

If shade houses are used, an even more open mix will prove beneficial. This will prevent rain from waterlogging the compost, a condition which Cymbidiums – in fact, any orchid – will not tolerate. A bark-based compost will reduce any risk of rotting.

REPOTTING

Cymbidiums will benefit from being repotted every alternate year or more frequently if the plant has deteriorated due to fungal infections or if rotting has occurred with overwatering.

After removing the plant from the pot, shake off any excess compost, especially if this has begun to decompose. A close inspection of the roots will then indicate the general condition of the plant. If the roots are firm to the touch and tightly entwined, the plant is healthy and will only need to be potted into the next size of pot.

Crocks or polystyrene chips may be placed at the bottom of a clean pot to assist with extra drainage. A light covering of compost should then be put on top. Position the plant centrally in the pot and gently add the fresh, dampened compost. Make sure there are no large unfilled cavities, but do not compress the compost too densely.

old plant must then be discarded, together with any decaying root matter, to eliminate the risk of bacterial/fungal infections. However, any plant suffering from ill-health should be repotted at once. All yellowing leaves must be removed from the plants, because their presence could cause serious fungal, bacterial and disease-related problems.

Cool-growing orchids

CYMBIDIUMS. Cymbidiums are possibly the best known and most widely grown of all orchids. They occur naturally throughout the Far East, from China and Japan, through the Himalayas and South-east Asia in the islands of the Philippines and as far south as Australia. They will survive happily in almost any place where the summers are warm and bright and the autumn and winter nights are sufficiently cool.

When growing Cymbidiums in temperate and sub-tropical climates it is beneficial to stand them outdoors in the early summer in a semi-shaded and preferably protected position. Later in the year, before any risk of frost occurs, they should be returned to a cool greenhouse, ideally heated to a minimum night temperature of 52–55°F (11–13°C).

ABOVE LEFT: Mini Cymbidium
Sarah Jean × Mdme
d'Estang.

ABOVE RIGHT: *Cymbidium
seedlings flowering for the first
time.*

RIGHT: *Healthy Cymbidium
root structure.*

If you discover, when you remove the plant from its old pot, that the root ball falls away or has rotted, first trim off all dead or badly damaged roots. Choose a clean pot into which the prepared plant will fit comfortably, and lightly pot it up with the dampened compost.

Always avoid over-potting – that is, repotting in too large a pot. This will not encourage new growth, and often increases the risk of rotting.

A Cymbidium plant sometimes becomes fairly large, and you may be inclined to divide or split it. However, always bear in mind that the larger the plant, the more flower spikes you can expect.

FEEDING AND WATERING

Do not water a newly potted plant immediately. Leave it until the compost is almost dry, possibly up to two or even three weeks. This will encourage new roots to grow into the fresh compost.

To start with, use only plain water until new root growth is evident. You can check this by gently tipping the plant out of the pot. Only then should any fertilizers be added to the water.

A normal watering and feeding programme can then be planned which relates to your growing conditions and the potting mix you have used. If a strong feed is given too early, the immature roots will undoubtedly burn and the plant will be substantially set back.

It is recommended that commercial fertilizers should always be used at half the stipulated strength. In many countries, manufacturers are not required to indicate the exact contents of their products on the container. Most fertilizers will have the general balance or proportions of the ingredients printed on the label, indicating relatively how much nitrogen (N), phosphorus (P) and potash (K) there is.

HUMIDITY AND SHADING

Cymbidiums will suffer less dehydration and stress if adequate humidity is maintained to prevent the pseudo-bulbs from shrivelling, especially in the summer months. In controlled glasshouses, humidity may be monitored more easily by constant damping of the pathways on sunny days.

In open shade houses, an overhead misting will help to lower leaf temperatures and, at the same time, raise humidity levels. Plants which are kept indoors should be placed on damp pebbles in trays, ensuring that the pots are not standing directly in water.

Summer shading is essential for Cymbidiums, especially in the sunnier tropical and semi-tropical countries. The leaves will scorch in direct sunlight, so it is necessary to use at least a 50 to 70 per cent shade-cloth. Too much shading, however, will inhibit the plants from flowering to their full potential, if at all.

RIGHT: *Cymbidium pot plant production nursery.*

BELOW: Mini Cymbidium Strathbraan *'Cooksbridge Purity'*.

BOTTOM: Mini Cymbidium Strathbraan *'Ditchling'*.

Lath houses are also used in some warmer climates to reduce the amount of light on the plants. They also allow good ventilation around the sides, which are left open. Ventilation is essential to ensure healthy plants. It is especially vital in the early evening and at night in the late summer months, when the temperature must be lowered to encourage the development of the flower spikes.

Avoid overcrowding the plants, as this leads to pests and diseases being passed rapidly from plant to plant. It also restricts the supply of air and light to the plant, and this will certainly reduce its chances of flowering.

ODONTOGLOSSUMS AND ALLIED GENERA.

Odontoglossums originate in Latin America, from Mexico in the north to Brazil in the south. They are found particularly in the mountainous regions of the Andes, mainly between 8,000 and 10,000 ft (roughly 2,500 to 3,000 m), although some do occur as high as 12,000 ft (3,658 m). The species are generally considered to be cool-growing, with only a few exceptions preferring intermediate conditions.

THE GROWING MEDIUM

Odontoglossums like an open compost that always retains a good percentage of air, even when the plant has been watered. An ideal compost for these delightful plants contains husky, fibrous peat or bark with added perlite. New Zealand chopped tree-fern fibre mixed with perlite in a proportion of 3:1 has proved to be an amazingly successful potting medium that spurs the plants to begin to root almost at once. Old root growth has also been seen to produce new branched roots, and much stronger, thicker roots have been observed to emerge from the base of the new growth. Charcoal should be avoided. Experience has shown that, when added to many mixes, it attracts any mineral salts which have not been leached out to form the white, chalky deposits often seen in pots.

The pH of the compost – that is, its relative acidity or alkalinity – should be adjusted so that it is just slightly acid. This means a reading of about 6 on the pH scale, where 7 indicates a neutral medium. This can be achieved by adding ground chalk (calcium carbonate) and dolomite or lime. The chalk not only helps to modify the pH but also provides an important, but often forgotten, element for plant growth – calcium. The dolomite also adjusts the pH, while at the same time providing additional magnesium.

REPOTTING

Repotting should be done every year, preferably after the plants have flowered, and ideally when the new growth is about 2 in (5 cm) high. Spring and autumn are the best times to repot. The summer months and any other hot periods of the year should be avoided.

ABOVE: *Shading is important for Odontoglossums, such as this* Odontoglossum crispum.

RIGHT: Odontioda Ingera *'Lyoth Galaxy'.*

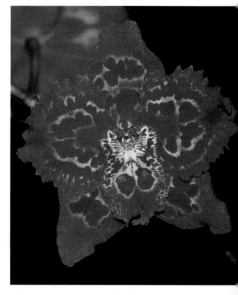

ABOVE: Odontioda (Ingera × Florence Sterling).

LEFT: Odontia (Mena × Wearside Galaxy).

BELOW: Odontoglossum pescatorei.

LEFT: Alexanderara St Ouen, *an Odontoglossum inter-generic hybrid.*

BELOW: Zygopetalum Mackayii – *unusually coloured and highly perfumed.*

First inspect the root ball, shake off any decaying compost and remove any dead roots. If the plant has too many old back bulbs without any root, one or two of these may be removed without harming the plant. Always be sure, however, to leave two bulbs with leaves and two older bulbs, because these will support the plant should it ever become stressed. At the end of each season all orchids will naturally lose a leaf or two from the oldest bulb.

Select a pot which will ideally accommodate one year's growth. Be sure to dampen the compost before potting and do not compress it too heavily in the pot around the new plant.

FEEDING AND WATERING

Like many orchids, Odontoglossums have pseudo-bulbs in which moisture and nutrients are stored. The plant will normally only draw on these resources when it becomes stressed due to lack of water or when producing a flower spike which it cannot support with its normal water and nutrient uptake. The compost should therefore never be allowed to become so dry that the bulb shrivels. It should be left, however, until it is holding only a small amount of water before giving it a thorough soaking.

More frequent watering will be necessary during the summer months. At this time the glasshouse should be well ventilated, and the plant will be in active growth and losing water through its leaves by transpiration. The plant should never be allowed to become waterlogged, as this will rot the root structure.

Odontoglossums are not lovers of fertilizer in high concentrations. This should be given at about a quarter to half strength. Although it may seem difficult to understand, it is often necessary to apply fertilizer at lower concentrations during the summer, especially in warm weather. The reason is that at this time the plants can be watered more frequently, and that more water is needed to replace that lost through transpiration. (See page 41 for details of fertilizers for different seasons.) At least once a month the plants must be watered

heavily without fertilizer to wash out any mineral salts which have accumulated in the compost.

TEMPERATURE, HUMIDITY AND SHADING

Odontoglossums thrive in conditions with high humidity almost throughout the year. Together with correct watering, high humidity will certainly prevent the pseudo-bulbs from shrivelling dramatically in the summer, a tendency to which they are prone.

A maximum summer temperature of 75–80°F (24–27°C) will suit these cool-growing orchids, but temperatures much higher will reduce their chances of flowering to their best. Experience has shown that, even in high daytime temperatures, the plants will not suffer unduly, providing they are healthy and have good root systems. In winter, a minimum temperature of about 50°F (10°C) is ideal. Although the plants will tolerate lower temperatures, great care with watering will be necessary in these circumstances.

Shading is essential during the summer. If the plants show any red pigmentation in their leaves, it is a sure sign that light levels are too high, although sometimes the cause may be found in the plant's nutrition.

If temperatures in the summer exceed 80°F (27°C), extra shading, ventilation and damping of the floors will be necessary.

Intermediate house orchids

PAPHIOPEDILUMS. Paphiopedilums – or Cypripediums, as they were known at the turn of the century – belong to the sub-tribe of the *Orchidaceae* family known as *Cypripediinae*. There are three other members: Cypripediums and Selenipediums from North America, Europe and the Far East, and Phragmipediums from South America. The Paphiopedilums occur naturally in South-east Asia, in an area stretching from New Guinea and the Philippines to China and India. Some of these are found at higher altitudes, and in cultivation they may tolerate slightly cooler conditions. It is generally the green-leaved plants which fall into this category, while the attractive mottle-leaved kinds require warmer, more tropical conditions. Paphiopedilums are curious plants which are often, incorrectly, thought to be carnivorous, because of the intriguing pouch that forms part of the flower. This is, in fact, merely a device to attract unsuspecting pollinators.

Paphiopedilums have proved to be worthwhile indoor pot plants which will flower annually given adequate attention. They have also come to be especially prized by collectors. Serious buyers are willing to pay large sums for choice clones which are rare or have received awards. This is largely due to the fact that it has not been possible to reproduce Paphiopedilums by tissue culture in great quantities. They can only be raised from seed or divided. However, Japanese and other scientists are working on techniques which will enable the plants to be multiplied on a mass-produced basis.

THE GROWING MEDIUM

Paphiopedilums are grown in a variety of media, ranging from bark mixtures, coconut chunks and fibres to peat concoctions, chopped sphagnum moss, osmunda fibre and tree-fern fibre. They will, in fact, grow successfully in almost any compost which is free-draining, yet able to retain enough moisture for their needs. Sandy loams and garden soil, however, are not recommended, even though Paphiopedilums are semi-terrestrials. Leaf mould has occasionally been added, but this is not essential. Whatever recipe you use, these orchids will benefit from the addition of ground chalk and dolomitic lime to the compost.

ABOVE: Paphiopedilum Black Rook *'Sussex Devine'*.

RIGHT: Phragmipedilum Grande, *a member of the sub-tribe Cypripediliinae.*

REPOTTING

Mature Paphiopedilums are very responsive to being repotted annually, and young seedlings twice a year. If a plant is in poor health or is seen to be producing many new growths, the chances are that it has few live roots, probably because of toxic compost, and repotting must be done immediately.

FEEDING AND WATERING

Paphiopedilums do not possess pseudo-bulbs like many other orchids, but use their somewhat fleshy leaves for storing nutrients. The compost must therefore be kept moist at all times, but should never be allowed to become waterlogged, as this will inevitably cause basal rot and the loss of root growth. Crocks or polystyrene chips in the base of the pots will assist in draining the pots.

High concentrations of fertilizers are likely to be detrimental to Paphiopedilums in cultivation, as they will tolerate only very weak solutions of feed at frequent intervals.

LEFT: *Nursery raised Paphiopedilums.*

RIGHT: Miltonia Many Waters 'Robin'. *Miltonias make excellent pot plants and are grown indoors with ease.*

BELOW: Miltonia 'Hamburg'

HUMIDITY AND SHADING

Paphiopedilums are shade-loving plants which will not tolerate excessively high light levels. Too much shade, however, will prevent them from blooming. They should be given adequate shade when grown in glasshouses and shade houses, especially in the summer, and ideally be sited away from direct sunlight when cultivated indoors. In order to lengthen the stems of Paphiopedilums some shading is necessary during the autumn.

Ventilation is vital and will reduce any risk of bacterial or fungal infections, especially if the plants are watered from overhead. Adequate humidity will keep the plants free of any dehydrating effects caused by dry breezes and heat in the summer and by internal heating when the plants are kept indoors.

MILTONIAS.

Well-grown Miltonias never cease to delight, producing enchanting, colourful flowers in profusion.

There are two sections within the Miltonia group: the warmth-tolerant Brazilian types, which tend to have starry flowers, and the cooler-growing Colombian varieties, which are known as Miltoniopsis and produce rounder, flat flowers in striking colours. Here both Miltonias and Miltoniopsis are grouped together, with specific references as needed.

Miltoniopsis were once believed to be very seasonal in their flowering habits, blooming mostly in late spring and early summer. However, a new strain has now been bred which, while producing lots of flowers at the normal time, will also bloom throughout the year.

THE GROWING MEDIUM

Miltonias like an open compost that does not hold excessive amounts of water. Punga, or New Zealand tree-fern fibre, mixed with perlite has recently been used with encouraging results. Peat, perlite and bark composts, however, have been positively tried and tested over a long period of time.

REPOTTING

Repotting should be carried out annually, although constant dividing is not desirable. As with all orchids, the roots must first be inspected for any dead or rotting roots, which must be removed. The prepared plant should then be potted into as small a pot as possible with fresh, dampened compost. The Miltonia types will eventually make superb specimen plants if they are potted on and not divided.

FEEDING

All Miltonias need to be fed regularly with half-strength nitrogenous fertilizers throughout the spring and summer, and with a potash-based feed in the autumn, which will prepare and harden the plants for winter.

Three colourful Cattleya varieties: (above) Sophrolaeliocattleya Dixie Jewels 'Suzuki' FCC/AOS; (left) Sophrolaeliocattleya Jewellers Art; and (below left) Laeliocattleya Petticoats 'Blumen Insel'.

HUMIDITY AND SHADING

The Miltonia types thrive in intermediate climatic conditions and require a fairly well-lit position. Miltoniopsis, however, need to be semi-shaded so that the attractive blue-green foliage does not get scorched. An average humidity of about 60 per cent, especially in the summer, will help prevent the pseudo-bulbs from shrivelling. A light overhead misting will, in addition, reduce the leaf temperature in very warm conditions and prevent the leaves from being caught up or 'concertinaed' when they emerge.

CATTLEYAS.
Cattleyas belong to a group which is the most flamboyant and colourful of all orchids. They came originally from various climatic regions of South America. They are a fairly permissive group, in the sense that they will cross with many genera which have similar structures and a range of interesting and often unique characteristics. These include such well-known genera as Brassavola (Rhyncholaelia), Laelia and Sophronitis. Brassavolas are sought after for their attractive, frilled labellums; Laelias are useful for adding extra stem length to the progeny, as well as increasing the number of flowers; and Sophronitis have the capacity to pass on their tolerance to cool conditions and their miniature characteristics. The list of cross-breeding genera is substantial, Epidendrum, Broughtonia and Barkeria often being used to produce inter-generic hybrids.

THE GROWING MEDIUM

Cattleyas particularly like a very free-draining compost containing at least 50 per cent bark. Extra drainage crocks are beneficial, especially to growers who water especially generously.

In Hawaii, some growers use very fibrous compost with great success, mainly due to the high humidity, which tends to reduce the frequency of watering. Some commercial growers prefer bark-based composts, others chopped coconut shells. All of these growing media prove highly acceptable.

RIGHT: Barkeria skinneri, *a variety often used to produce inter-generic hybrids.*

BELOW: Sophrolaeliocattleya Hazel Boyd '*Splash*'.

REPOTTING

The best time to repot Cattleyas is when the new growth has appeared and just before it begins to produce new roots, normally in the spring.

Remove the plant and shake off any excess compost. If the roots are in good condition and still firm, it can be planted into the next size pot with fresh, damp compost added to secure it. In warm conditions, if bark-based compost is used, it should be soaked in water for a week before potting and then,

after planting, be left to dry. During this drying-out period the newly potted plant will rapidly produce new roots.

If the plant to be repotted has few roots, or is a division or even a recently imported plant, it is quite possible that the root growth will be damaged or dehydrated. In this case, it should be potted as usual in fresh, damp compost, but then left to dry out before any more water is given.

To support divisions of plants with few roots, a bamboo cane or wire stake must be inserted into the pot as close as possible to the oldest pseudo-bulb. A firm tie should then be made at the base, below the leaf, using garden string or plastic twist tie. The stake should hold the plant firmly in place and should only be removed when enough new roots have emerged.

As alternatives to potting, Cattleya plants can be mounted on to an attractive piece of driftwood or planted in decorative, hanging slatted baskets. If a plant is to be mounted, some sphagnum moss should be placed between it and the wood in order to hold some moisture. Otherwise, the plant will dry out rapidly if there is insufficient humidity. Use either a staple gun to staple over the rhizome and into the wood, or, if available, a nylon stocking. By the time the plant has adhered itself to its host, the staple should have rusted away, or the stocking disintegrated. Broughtonias, which are notoriously poor growers in pots, will happily thrive in this manner.

FEEDING AND WATERING

During the hotter months of the year, Cattleyas need to be watered frequently. Always make sure, however, that the compost has dried to some extent, but not completely. Gradually reduce the watering as the cooler months approach, and in winter follow the rule that it is probably safer not to water than to water.

This 'drying-off' period will have the effect of discouraging winter growth, which tends to be weak and sometimes spindly. New growth enticed in the spring, on the other hand, will have the advantage of stronger light, which will enable it to mature during the summer months.

Throughout the late spring and summer, well-rooted plants can be given regular feeds of nitrogen-based fertilizers at half the recommended strength at alternate waterings. But water heavily without fertilizer at least once a month to remove any harmful deposits of mineral salts left by the feeds in the compost.

TEMPERATURE, HUMIDITY AND SHADING

The Cattleya types thrive in semi-shaded positions in warm and sunny, tropical and sub-tropical climates. The hybrids, however, will generally grow quite happily in intermediate conditions if given a well-lit situation. In temperate climates, a heated glasshouse will be necessary. The ideal temperature range for the Cattleya group is between 58 and 85°F (14–29°C), although higher temperatures are tolerated for short periods in the summer.

Humidity is of vital importance at this time, to reduce any further loss of moisture from the pseudo-bulbs and fleshy leaves. During this time, much of the plant may be exposed to fairly strong light, so the humidity must be kept constant and

LEFT: Sophrolaeliocattleya Mine Gold.

ABOVE: Cattleyonia Why Not.

ABOVE: Brassolaeliocattleya
Rangers Six 'A–OK'.

RIGHT: Brassolaeliocattleya
Golden Jubilee.

additional light mistings given to help to reduce shrivelling. In excessive periods of heat, the plant will undoubtedly begin to suffer. In these circumstances, the floor of the growing area should be dampened and the shading and ventilation increased to reduce the temperature. Evaporative cooling systems are very useful for this purpose. They draw air through wet pads into the glasshouse, reducing the inside temperature and increasing the humidity. Such systems are not effective, however, in warm climates which have high natural humidity.

CALANTHES. Calanthes are divided into two groups: deciduous and evergreen. The deciduous group contains some of the first orchids to be cultivated in Britain and the first to be successfully crossed by the adventurous Scottish gardener John Dominy. The species were collected from the Himalayas and areas of Burma and Thailand.

After flowering, the bulbs of deciduous Calanthes should be allowed to rest in intermediate conditions, without water but receiving as much light as possible. Once the new growths have begun to emerge, much of the old root should be removed, leaving only enough to secure the bulbs after repotting.

Recommended for this purpose is a peat-based compost with added perlite or seedling bark in a proportion of 2:1. The bulbs should be firmly planted in the dampened mix in small pots, preferably with crocks added, and placed in a light aspect.

The pots should not be watered until the roots have begun to infiltrate the new compost, and even then sparingly. When

ABOVE AND LEFT: Calanthe Bryan *and* Calanthe Grouville *'Red Baron', two deciduous varieties.*

the new growths are almost 6 in (15 cm) long, the plant can be watered properly. A nitrogenous feed must also be introduced at the same time. Toward autumn, the flower spikes will begin to emerge and the foliage to turn yellow. A potash-based feed must then be given and the water gradually reduced until the leaves have fallen. If the plants are being kept in a greenhouse, no more water will be required, even if the plants are in flower.

Tropical house orchids

PHALAENOPSIS. Phalaenopsis, the pride of the tropical Asian jungles, are orchids which do not possess pseudo-bulbs, but store nutrients and moisture in their firm, fleshy leaves. There are about 70 species in all, ranging throughout the Far East from Malaysia to Taiwan and from the Philippines to New Guinea.

Doritis is allied to Phalaenopsis and can be cultivated in the same way.

THE GROWING MEDIUM
An open compost is recommended for these orchids consisting of 50 per cent chunky bark added to a peat base and perlite. Heavy waterers should increase the bark content so that too much water is not retained by the compost. Charcoal is often used in many Phalaenopsis compost recipes, but care must be taken as mineral salts will be attracted to it.

REPOTTING
Repotting should ideally be carried out after flowering during spring or summer using fresh, damp compost. After removing the plant from the pot, the root ball must be inspected and any roots showing signs of damage or rotting must be trimmed. Loosely fill the pot around the roots with fresh compost, and water only when new root tips have begun to penetrate it.

FEEDING AND WATERING
The fleshy leaves of Phalaenopsis are used to store moisture, and for this reason the plants must never be allowed to become too dry without giving them adequate humidity. As a general rule, however, they should be on the point of drying out before they are re-watered. Never let them become waterlogged as this will undoubtedly cause rotting, first to the roots and finally the whole plant.

Phalaenopsis require constant feeds at half the strength recommended for commercial fertilizers. They should also be given at least one heavy watering a month to ensure that mineral salt deposits are leached out of the pots.

TEMPERATURE, HUMIDITY AND SHADING
Phalaenopsis are ideal house plants when given a warm atmosphere, a minimum night temperature of 60°F (15°C) and adequate humidity during the day. As they are generally

FACING PAGE: Phalaenopsis Orchid World *'Our Planet'*.

RIGHT: Phalaenopsis (Golden Buddah × Golden Pride).

BELOW: Phalaenopsis (Jungle Ruby × javanica).

BOTTOM: Phalaenopsis schilleriana. *This specimen was growing in a private garden in Quezon, Philippines.*

epiphytic by nature and can be seen in the wild clinging to tree branches, they are naturally kept in the shade for much of the year. When cultivated in greenhouses, therefore, they need extra shading, more so in the summer than in the winter. When indoors, the plants should be kept away from direct sunlight but placed in an aspect where they will receive diffused indirect light.

As for any orchid, ventilation is essential for Phalaenopsis to refresh the atmosphere around the plants. This will also assist in reducing the humidity after the plants have been watered, helping to dry them out. Ideally, there should be no visible moisture on the foliage by the end of the day, as this can cause fungal and bacterial rots which can often destroy a plant. By sunset, if any moisture is still present, the night temperature should be increased to between 65 and 68°F (18–20°C). An oscillating fan will assist in drying off any excess moisture. These problems, however, can be avoided by watering as early as possible in the morning.

When used as house plants, Phalaenopsis should be stood on damp gravel trays to provide humidity around the leaves. On a hot day a fine mist may be sprayed over the leaves to reduce further dehydration. The leaves may also be wiped down with a damp cloth from time to time to remove any dust that may have settled.

ABOVE: Arachnis Maggie Oei,
part of the clan associated with
the Vanda family (described on
page 39).

FACING PAGE, ABOVE:
Dendrobium 'Lava Flow'.

FACING PAGE, BELOW:
Dendrobium Phalaenopsis
hybrid.

DENDROBIUMS. One of the largest groups of
orchid sub-tribes is the Dendrobium family, which contains
more than 1,500 distinct species and possibly thousands of
hybrids. Most of the species occur in the Far East, a vast area
stretching from Malaysia to Korea, eastward through New
Guinea into the Pacific islands of Polynesia, and southward to
Australia and New Zealand. The species grow in a variety of
climates and at different altitudes.

Dendrobium plants vary in size, some being smaller than a
matchbox, others large, robust specimens measuring over 3 ft
(1 m). They are epiphytic by nature and, in general, enjoy
good light and ventilation. Because of the complexity of this
genus, some varieties may prove to be shy to flower. In these
cases, their position should be changed for a season to coax
them to bloom.

DENDROBIUM TYPES

It is necessary to differentiate between the types of
Dendrobium which have become commercially viable and are
easy to cultivate, and the more difficult varieties, which are
merely chanced by the most enthusiastic collectors.

GROUP 1

The soft-cane varieties or *Dendrobium nobile* types, are
easy to cultivate in extremely well-draining composts in either
pots or hanging baskets. Chopped tree-fern fibre mixed with
perlite, or a very open, bark-based compost are acceptable as a
medium to these types of Dendrobium.

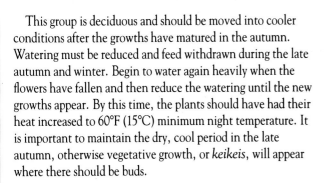

This group is deciduous and should be moved into cooler conditions after the growths have matured in the autumn. Watering must be reduced and feed withdrawn during the late autumn and winter. Begin to water again heavily when the flowers have fallen and then reduce the watering until the new growths appear. By this time, the plants should have had their heat increased to 60°F (15°C) minimum night temperature. It is important to maintain the dry, cool period in the late autumn, otherwise vegetative growth, or *keikeis*, will appear where there should be buds.

GROUP 2

The second group, which includes *Dendrobium parishii*, thrives in conditions suitable for Cattleyas throughout the year, but with a slightly drier autumn. By this time the growths have matured and the leaves have begun to fall.

GROUP 3

In this group are *Dendrobium thyrsiflorum* and *D. densiflorum*. These are evergreen and do not require a drying-off period like other groups of Dendrobiums. They will tolerate Phalaenopsis conditions all year round and reliably reward the grower with cascading lanterns of colourful flowers.

GROUP 4

Many of the evergreen Philippine Dendrobiums require night temperatures of around 60°F (15°C) and warm, sunny days. A short dry period in the late autumn is needed to mature the hard canes of this group.

The Phalaenopsis Dendrobium group should have their watering restricted after the growths have matured and before new growth appears. This evergreen group is more tolerant of shade and ideally suits general Phalaenopsis conditions.

SUMMARY OF CULTURAL CONDITIONS

All Dendrobium types prefer open composts of either tree-fern fibre and perlite or bark-based peat. Whichever medium is used, it must be open enough to maintain some air around the roots. Dendrobiums may be grown in baskets or pots, or on tree-fern slabs, and repotting and dividing should be done only when new growths begin to appear. Care with watering is essential. Dendrobiums cannot tolerate wet, soggy composts, which will inevitably damage and rot their wiry roots. Occasional mistings on the foliage will help any moisture loss occurring during very warm days in tropical and sub-tropical climates.

Dendrobiums can be propagated by cutting the old canes between the sections and laying them on fresh, damp compost. Plantlets will quickly develop at the nodes.

VANDAS. Vandas, from the heart of Asia, are very rewarding orchids, which produce long-lasting sprays of flowers in warmer climates. Sadly, the species and hybrids can be flowered only with difficulty in conditions where light intensity is lower than in tropical climates.

Ascocentrums are closely related to the Vanda family, and are noted for their miniature forms and bright colours. Aerides, Arachnis, Euanthes and Renantheras are also members of the clan which are used to produce intergeneric hybrids within this group.

CULTURAL CONDITIONS

In tropical and sub-tropical climates the Vanda and Ascocentrum families can be seen thriving outdoors basking in brilliant sunshine. In cultivation, however, care should be taken to protect them from intense heat and light.

Maximum ventilation at times of high temperatures will assist in cooling the leaves. High summer humidity will also keep the leaves firm, as will fairly heavy waterings during the growing season.

Vandas are extremely heavy feeders, so regular applications of nitrogenous fertilizers at half strength will be beneficial. They adapt well to being grown in various media. They will accept sawdust, bark, or even beds of broken bricks or wooden slatted baskets, so long as the medium is extremely porous. Long roots will be produced by the plants, and total exposure to the air will not harm them.

OTHER TROPICAL ORCHIDS. A number of other interesting epiphytic orchids are easy to grow in intermediate to warm conditions similar to those suitable for Phalaenopsis but with slightly more light. Cyrtorchis, Mystacidium, Neofinetia and Angraecum are included in this group. Many varieties within these genera can be grown successfully when mounted on wood, tree-fern poles or slabs, or cork blocks.

FACING PAGE: Vanda Miss Joachim *var.* alba.

RIGHT: *A Vanda specimen.*

EASY REFERENCE CULTURE TABLES

Paphiopedilums

SEASON	SPRING			SUMMER			AUTUMN			WINTER			
Ideal Day Temp.	21 70	21 70	24 75	24 75	24 75	24 75	24 75	21 70	20 68	20 68	20 68	20 68	degrees C degrees Fahr.
Ideal Night Temp.	16 60	16 60	16 60	16 60	16 60	16 60	16 60	16 60	14 58	14 58	14 58	14 58	degrees C degrees Fahr.
Watering	L/F	F	F	F	F	F	F	L/F	L	L	L	L	F – frequent L – less freq.
Feeding	N	N	N	N/G	G/N	N	K	N	G	G	G	G	N – high Nitrogen G – General Feed K – Potassium
Shading	L/H	H	H	H	H	H	H	L/H	L	N	N	L	N – no shading L – light shading H – heavy shading
Ventilation	L/M	M	M	M	M	M	M	L/M	L	L	L	L	M – more L – less
Humidity	H	H	H	H	H	H	H	H	H/L	H/L	H/L	H	H – high L – low
Repotting	Y	N	N	N	N	N	Y	N	N	N	Y	Y	Y – yes N – no

Miltonias

SEASON	SPRING			SUMMER			AUTUMN			WINTER			
Ideal Day Temp.	21 70	21 70	24 75	24 75	24 75	24 75	24 75	21 70	20 68	20 68	20 68	20 68	degrees C degrees Fahr.
Ideal Night Temp.	16 60	16 60	16 60	16 60	16 60	16 60	16 60	16 60	14 58	14 58	14 58	14 58	degrees C degrees Fahr.
Watering	F	F	F	F	F	F	F	L/F	L	L	L	L/F	F – frequent L – less freq.
Feeding	N	N	N	N	N	N	K	N	G	G	G	G	N – high Nitrogen G – General Feed K – Potassium
Shading	L/H	H	H	H	H	H	H	L/H	L	N	N	L	N – no shading L – light shading H – heavy shading
Ventilation	L/M	M	M	M	M	M	M	L/M	L	L	L	L	M – more L – less
Humidity	H	H	H	H	H	H	H	H	H/L	H/L	H/L	H	H – high L – low
Repotting	Y	Y	N	N	N	N	Y	Y	N	N	N	N	Y – yes N – no

Phalaenopsis

SEASON	SPRING			SUMMER			AUTUMN			WINTER			
Ideal Day Temp.	24 75	24 75	24 75	27 80	27 80	27 80	24 75	24 75	24 75	24 75	24 75	24 75	degrees C degrees Fahr.
Ideal Night Temp.	18 65	18 65	18 65	20 68	20 68	20 68	18 65	18 65	18 65	18 65	18 65	18 65	degrees C degrees Fahr.
Watering	L/F	L/F	F	F	F	F	L/F	L/F	L	L	L	L	F – frequent L – less freq.
Feeding	N	N	N	N	N	N	K	N	G	G	G	G	N – high Nitrogen G – General Feed K – Potassium
Shading	L/H	L/H	H	H	H	H	H	L/H	L	N	N	L	N – no shading L – light shading H – heavy shading
Ventilation	L	L/M	M	M	M	M	M	L/M	L	L	L	L	M – more L – less
Humidity	H/L	H/L	H	H	H	H	H/L	H/L	L	L	L	L	H – high L – low
Repotting	Y	Y	N	N	N	N	N	N	N	N	N	Y	Y – yes N – no

Cattleyas

SEASON	SPRING			SUMMER			AUTUMN			WINTER			
Ideal Day Temp.	24 75	27 80	27 80	29 85	29 85	29 85	27 80	27 80	24 75	21 70	21 70	21 70	degrees C degrees Fahr.
Ideal Night Temp.	16 60	16 60	16 60	17 62	17 62	17 62	16 60	16 60	16 60	14 58	14 58	14 58	degrees C degrees Fahr.
Watering	L/F	L/F	F	F	F	F	L/F	L/F	L/F	L	L	L	F – frequent L – less freq.
Feeding	G	N	N	N	N	N	K	G	G	G	G	G	N – high Nitrogen G – General Feed K – Potassium
Shading	N	L	L	L	L	L	L	N	N	N	N	N	N – no shading L – light shading H – heavy shading
Ventilation	L	L/M	M	M	M	M	M	M/L	L	L	L	L	M – more L – less
Humidity	H/L	H/L	H	H	H	H	H	H	H/L	L	L	L	H – high L – low
Repotting	Y	Y	Y	Y	N	N	N	N	N	N	N	N	Y – yes N – no

Cymbidiums

SEASON	SPRING			SUMMER			AUTUMN			WINTER			
Ideal Day Temp.	21 70	21 70	21 70	24 75	27 80	27 80	24 75	21 70	18 65	18 65	18 65	18 65	degrees C degrees Fahr.
Ideal Night Temp.	11 52	13 55	16 60	16 60	16 60	16 60	13 55	13 55	11 52	11 52	11 52	11 52	degrees C degrees Fahr.
Watering	L/F	L/F	F	F	F	F	L/F	L/F	L	L	L	L	F – frequent L – less freq.
Feeding	N	N	N	N	G	G	K	G	G	G	G	G	N – high Nitrogen G – General Feed K – Potassium
Shading	L	L	H	H	H	H	H/L	L	N	N	N	L	N – no shading L – light shading H – heavy shading
Ventilation	L	M	M	M	M	M	M	L	L	L	L	L	M – more L – less
Humidity	L	H/L	H	H	H	H	H	H/L	L	L	L	L	H – high L – low
Repotting	Y	Y	Y	Y	N	N	N	N	N	N	N	N	Y – yes N – no

Odontoglossums

SEASON	SPRING			SUMMER			AUTUMN			WINTER			
Ideal Day Temp.	18 65	21 70	21 70	24 75	24 75	24 75	21 70	21 70	18 65	18 60	18 65	18 65	degrees C degrees Fahr.
Ideal Night Temp.	11 52	13 55	16 60	16 60	16 60	16 60	16 60	16 60	11 52	11 52	11 52	11 52	degrees C degrees Fahr.
Watering	L/F	L/F	F	F	F	F	L/F	L/F	L	L	L	L	F – frequent L – less freq.
Feeding	N	N	N	N	N	N	K	N	G	G	G	G	N – high Nitrogen G – General Feed K – Potassium
Shading	L/H	H	H	H	H	H	H	L/H	L	N	N	L	N – no shading L – light shading H – heavy shading
Ventilation	L/M	M	M	M	M	M	M	L/M	L	L	L	L	M – more L – less
Humidity	H	H	H	H	H	H	H	H	H/L	H/L	H/L	H	H – high L – low
Repotting	Y	Y	N	N	N	N	Y	Y	N	N	N	N	Y – yes N – no

MODERN PROPAGATION METHODS

O nce you have mastered the general requirements and life cycle of the orchid, you will find it relatively easy to grow these reasonably tough plants and perhaps even to breed your own hybrids. Breeding orchids is a fascinating and rewarding business, but it involves not only technical knowledge and skill but also some research into the genetic background of the plants you intend to use.

Selecting suitable parents

There are one or two points to bear in mind before you set about choosing plants for breeding. Certain criteria have to be satisfied to ensure you select suitable specimens.

1 You must first check the genus, the name and the varietal name of the plants you propose using as parents. From this information you can trace their parentage and family tree in order to see which hybrids and species appear in their background. At the same time you can check if your intended breeding plants have previously been used with consistently good results. If they are themselves the result of careful line breeding, they will very likely prove to be rewarding parents.

2 You need to be clear about your objectives in advance. Do you want the new hybrid for exhibition purposes, or for ordinary decorative use? Are you aiming to produce a pot plant, or a collector's plant prized perhaps for its rarity value or intended, as in some cases, for raising a new inter-generic group – that is, a new genus from two different genera?

3 The specimens you have selected should be free-flowering and easy growing, as this will obviously add vigour to their progeny and help in cultivation. The flowers, coloration and spike habit should all have an appealing impact. Finally, and of utmost importance, the plants must have clean foliage and be free of any virus, disease, or any genetic abnormality.

4 It is important to know something of the chromosome make-up of the parent plants you have selected for breeding as this will have a direct bearing on their suitability. Plants with two sets of chromosomes in their cells, known as *diploids*, generally grow easily and breed well. *Triploids*, plants which have three sets of chromosomes, are usually easy growers and free-flowering and produce larger flowers than diploids, but they do not usually breed. Triploids are usually the result of mating a diploid with a tetraploid. *Tetraploids*, with four sets of chromosomes, generally have superior flowers to diploids, but are slower to mature and produce fewer flowers than either diploids or triploids. However, many superior hybrids have resulted from breeding programmes using tetraploids. Apart

ABOVE AND RIGHT: *Protocorm development and a single seed, as seen through the microscope.*

FACING PAGE: Odontioda (Ingmar × Heatonensis) 'Lyoth Glow'.

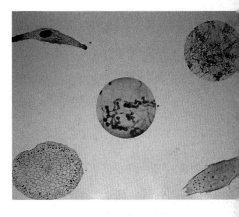

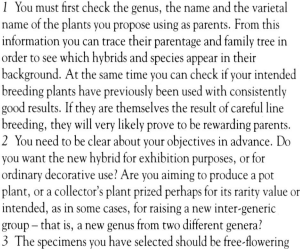

from triploids, other plants with unsuitable chromosome counts, or *ploidy*, for breeding purposes are those that are known to have odd counts, known as *aneuploids*.

5 Also to be rejected as possible parents are any seedlings which have been slow to mature or are susceptible to disease.

Pollination and seed production

When you have finally selected the parent plants you wish to use, you can then begin the process of cross-pollination. Use a toothpick carefully to remove the pollen cap and the pollinia from the pod parent – that is, the maternal plant that is to form the seed pod. This is to ensure that there is no possibility of self-pollination. Then remove the pollen cap from the paternal plant and the pollinia; gently press against the sticky surface of the stigma of the pod plant.

Soon after pollination the surface of the stigma swells over the pollen granules. The flower then begins to wilt. Within a week of pollination the column becomes slightly swollen and the ovary begins to enlarge. Fertilization, however, may take up to three months after pollination.

If, for some reason, the crossing has been incompatible, the seed capsule will begin to die and fall off. This may happen if the pollen or the pod parent is sterile; if there has been a dramatic change in temperature; if fungal or bacterial infection has damaged the flower parts; or if the pollen was not fresh enough.

LEFT: *Orchid seed*

BELOW: *Phalaenopsis seedlings in the flask.*

RIGHT: *Replated flask.*

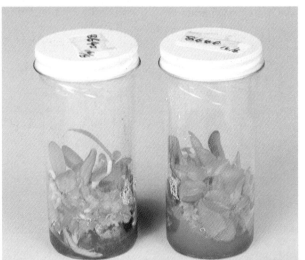

Seed is produced inside the pod over a period of time, which may be from four to 14 months for some genera. The pod may sometimes yield only a few seeds, sometimes hundreds, thousands, or occasionally millions in the case of some species. The pod is mature when it yellows and you can see cracks along the fluted sides. It should then be removed. It is also possible to remove the pod before it is mature, but this is not recommended as viral diseases may be passed on to the progeny.

Germination in sterile containers

When the first hybridizers started their breeding programmes, modern techniques of seed sowing were unknown. They merely scattered the seed around the mother plant. Not many of the seeds germinated, but the ones that did so usually grew into sturdy, vigorous plants.

Later, the technique of sowing the seed on a bed of sphagnum moss covered with a muslin cloth came into use. This was superseded in the late 1800s by another method still basically in use today. In this technique the seeds were germinated in sterile flasks containing a nutrient medium to support the orchid fungus. A necessary step forward came in the mid 1920s when Dr Lewis Knudson of Cornell University in the United States devised a formula to combine the plant nutrients with sugar as a carbohydrate source, and agar (see table opposite).

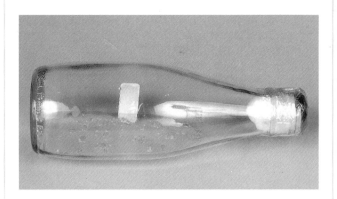

The process begins with the preparation of the nutrient recipe. Nowadays, the ingredients are available already mixed. Following the printed instructions, weigh out the chemical mix on a balance and add it to a beaker containing a measured quantity of distilled or purified water. Stir the solution thoroughly over a gentle heat until everything is dissolved. Pour the liquid to a depth of about ¾ in (2 cm) into flasks, bottles or other containers that will tolerate high temperatures and pressures in an *autoclave*, or pressure vessel. Plug the containers with stoppers or non-absorbent cotton wool and heat in an autoclave for between 15 and 20 minutes at 15 lb (6.8 kg) pressure. The nutrient solution will then be sterilized.

LEFT: Cattleya percivalliana
'Extra'.

ABOVE: *Cymbidium mericlones
in plastic containers.*

The Knudson 'C' Formula

CHEMICAL	AMOUNT
Calcium nitrate – $Ca(NO_3)_2 . 4H_2O$	1g
Magnesium sulphate – $MgSO_4 . 7H_2O$	250mg
Ammonium sulphate – $(NH_4)_2SO_4$	500mg
Potassium phosphate – KH_2PO_4	250mg
Ferrous sulphate – $FeSO_4 . 7H_2O$	25mg
Manganese sulphate – $MnSO_4 . 4H_2O$	7,5mg
Sucrose (sugar)	20g
Agar (amount needed depends on quality)	8–15g
Water (purified or distilled)	1000ml
(pH adjusted to 5 with Hydrochloric Acid)	

Originally published in the *American Orchid Society Bulletin* No.15 pp. 214–217 by Dr Lewis Knudson in 1946.

To sterilize the seed, place it in a test tube half filled with a 10 per cent solution of calcium hypochlorite which has been filtered. Shake vigorously for three minutes, then top up with more solution if necessary and leave to stand for one hour.

Dip a sterilized metal spatula into the seed, gathering as much as possible. Then insert it into the flask and spread the seed over the now solidified agar. Flame the cotton wool, place a plastic cover over it and secure it with adhesive tape.

The prepared flasks should then be stored at a temperature of about 70°F (21°C). They can be placed either in natural light or in special chambers with ordinary warm white fluorescent tubes suspended about 16 in (40 cm) above them.

Germination may take from a few days, in the case of Odontoglossums, up to several months for Cymbidiums and Paphiopedilums. The seed first begins to swell, then forms a globular mass of tissue called a *protocorm*. Root hairs then appear, and finally roots and leaf shoots. Unless they have been sown thinly, the plantlets will then need to be transplanted. The transplanting process must ensure that each seedling has sufficient space to develop until it can be removed from the sterile flask. For their final transplanting in flask, food additives such as liquidized banana are often added. At this stage a laminar flow cabinet or similar unit will be necessary to prevent contamination. A laminar flow cabinet will give a sterile work area by forcing air through filters.

After about eight to 12 months the plants should be sufficiently well established for them to be removed from the flasks.

LEFT: *Orchid plants potted singly.*

ABOVE RIGHT: *Cymbidium plants in community pots.*

BELOW RIGHT: *A laminar flow cabinet, as described on page 47*

FACING PAGE: Hazel Boyd 'Splash'

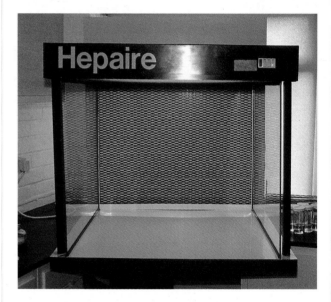

Planting out the seedlings

The best time to de-flask the young plants is either in the spring or early autumn. A seedling compost must first be prepared using finer grades of bark or peat, with the addition of perlite or similar material to ensure an open, free-draining medium.

Carefully remove the plants from the flask. Clean off as much of the gel as possible, and pot up, preferably in clumps. The young plantlets become established more quickly if planted fairly close together in a community pot. Water thoroughly with a mild fungicide or bactericide and place in a propagator or frame. This will ensure adequate humidity; the temperature should be kept between 65°F (18°C) at night and 80°F (27°C) during the day. Good ventilation is also important, and any plants affected by fungus or bacteria should be removed at once and a second dose of fungicide or bactericide applied.

Always allow the compost to dry slightly before re-watering, and wait until new roots have begun to develop before giving weak solutions of fertilizer. Use only water, however, at alternate waterings to prevent any build-up of mineral salts in the compost. This can prove disastrous to young seedlings.

After six months repot the plants again, this time singly, in fresh compost in suitably small pots. Continue to repot at regular intervals to help the plants to grow more quickly and to bring them into flower in the shortest time.

Micropropagation – the technique of tissue culture

Most orchids are *heterozygous* – that is, they will not breed true to type, so every plant will be different. Vegetative reproduction, which does give identical offspring, is a very slow process for most orchids, and only one, or possibly two, slow process for most orchids, and only one, or possibly two, divisions of the parent plant are possible each year. This made fine clones extremely expensive before the 1960s.

Fortunately, there were eminent biologists working in the field of propagation by *tissue culture*. The French biologist Georges Morel was one of the first to make a breakthrough which was to make the mass production of orchid plants possible. While working on a process to rid potatoes and dahlias of viruses, he turned his attention, being an orchid enthusiast, to the challenge of eradicating viruses from the orchids. Using his vast knowledge, he tried first to rid the world famous breeder *Cymbidium Alexanderi* 'Westonbirt' of its disease.

The technique Morel used involves taking a shoot from the mother plant and dissecting some of the outer leaves to expose the lateral buds. The shoot must then be sterilized in a 70 per cent alcohol solution and then a weak hypochlorite solution for a further 20 minutes. The lateral buds are then dissected under a microscope so that the tiny *apical meristem*, or

ABOVE: *Cymbidium mericlones flowering in a nursery.*

RIGHT: *Cattleya seedling to be used for tissue culture.*

BELOW: *Cymbidium tissue in the multiplication stage.*

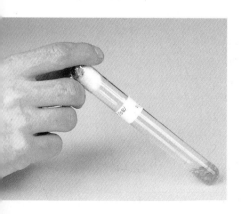

Reproductive organs before fertilization

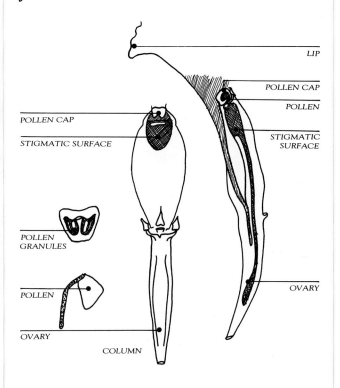

Reproductive organs after fertilization

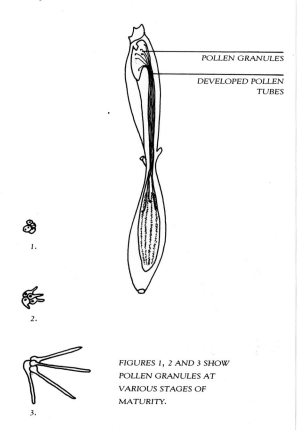

FIGURES 1, 2 AND 3 SHOW POLLEN GRANULES AT VARIOUS STAGES OF MATURITY.

growing tip, can be reached and cut out. This is placed in a sterilized flask containing a medium similar to that used for seed sowing but with added trace elements, vitamins and sometimes auxin or cytokinins. The flask is then placed in a room with controlled light and temperature conditions, as in the case of seed germination.

The tiny piece of tissue, about the size of a pinhead, produces a globular mass similar to the protocorm produced by a seed and is known as a PLB, or protocorm-like body. Morel discovered that this PLB produces a normal plantlet free of virus. Perhaps even more important was the discovery that if the PLB is damaged or sectioned, it will produce another PLB within weeks.

This means that the PLBs can be sectioned every four or five weeks, and they will proliferate and produce more PLBs. As soon as the chopping process stops, the PLBs begin to sprout leaves and roots and then following a similar pattern to that of seedling development.

A word of caution here: it is often written that all plants produced by this technique will be identical, but it has been observed that mutations can and do sometimes occur. However, it is possible to spot these mutations at an early stage and ensure that only plants of similar genetic makeup to the original are produced.

The tissue culture technique has proved to be the greatest breakthrough so far in the production of orchids. It has enabled extremely fine and often very rare orchids to become reasonably priced and available in quantity.

Propagation by division

When a Cymbidium plant gets to a reasonable size it can be propagated quite easily by *division*, or splitting it up. Make sure that each piece of the plant you select has at least two green bulbs (new growths) and two back bulbs (old growths). This will allow the new plant to draw sustenance from the old bulbs should it be necessary. Make the cut with a sharp knife which has been flamed to sterilize it and to ensure that no plant juices are transferred from one plant to another. Each cut should then be treated with a sealing agent or fungicide powder. Finally, pot the plants in a suitable growing medium To avoid disappointment it is worth remembering that the new plants may be disinclined to flower until the following season.

Any individual back bulbs left over after splitting up the original plant can be collected to grow even more new plants. Put them in a sealed plastic bag and hang them up, perhaps under the greenhouse staging. After a short time they will produce new growths and can be potted up in the usual way.

PESTS AND DISEASES

Although you may have the most perfect growing conditions, you can still be faced with an outbreak of disease or infestation of pests. However, the risk is greatly reduced if one is selective when purchasing new plants, and propagates only from healthy stock. It certainly is true that healthy, well-grown plants are much more resilient to disease.

Fungi and bacteria will normally affect only weakened plants, but the problem will also occur if the growing environment is not suitable. If your plants are suffering from this type of disease problem on a significant scale, reduce the humidity and watering frequency, and ventilate whenever possible. If necessary, spray with fungicide/bactericide. At this point you must consider whether the growing environment is suitable and make any changes necessary.

Hygiene in the greenhouse is essential. Ensure weeds are pulled out and all dead leaves from the plants removed. Never leave old dirty pots or compost lying around, as these will harbour and encourage infection. It is a good idea to have a periodic spring-clean, washing down the walls and floor of the greenhouse to eradicate lurking pests and potential disease. Also, algae should be removed as it makes the floor dangerously slippery when wet.

Orchids generally suffer from similar pests to those encountered on other plants. If you are unsure of the pest, disease or possible remedy, ask your nursery for advice.

Be practical when you notice an infestation for the first time. Before rushing for the insecticide, check the scale of the problem first. If possible, remove the pests by hand where the infestation is of a minor nature. Then, if it is worse than was first thought, use the insecticide. It is essential to follow the manufacturer's directions, as overdoses can damage your plants while too little may not eradicate the insects.

SAFETY WHEN USING CHEMICALS

- Always wear gloves to prevent contact with the chemicals.
- Be careful not to allow any contact with your face or body. In the event of contact, wash any chemicals off immediately.
- Only mix the quantity you need to use at the time.
- Store any chemicals well out of reach of children or pets.

It is now possible to obtain a range of natural predators which control many of the pests commonly encountered when growing orchids.

FACING PAGE: *Odontoglossum flowers showing greenfly.*

Orchids

PEST	CHARACTERISTICS/SYMPTOMS	REMEDY
Ants – small black or red insects.	Attracted by the secretion of liquid from the flowers, they transport and transfer aphids and scale insects. They also infest composts.	*A general insecticide will eradicate ants.*
Aphids (Greenfly) – small, plump flying insects.	These are attracted to young seedlings and emerging flower spikes, causing damage to the flowers. They leave messy secretions of honeydew which may attract ants and fungus.	*Remove minor infestations by hand; otherwise a general insecticide will eliminate these pests.*
Leaf Miner – small, white grubs.	These have been known to infect orchids, passing on virus-related diseases.	*Remove infected leaves and use a systemic pesticide.*
Mealy Bug – small, furry white sucking pest.	These bugs are usually found on the underside of leaves, in growing apexes and on new growth. They will attack most orchids.	*For mild infestations, cotton wool swabs and a very mild liquid detergent will remove the live adults. Then spray with Malathion or dimethoate.*
Red Spider Mite – minute orange-red spidery insect.	These pests produce fine webs on the underside of leaves, which later results in silvery scarred markings. Cymbidiums are especially prone to attack.	*Increased humidity will discourage these pests. Treat with a specific miticide.*
Scale – brown, scaly crusts.	These pests suck sap from the plant, leaving a dark, furry fungal-type residue and sticky honey-dew They also leave lighter coloured circular marks on upper leaves.	*Mild infestations may be wiped with cotton wool swabs soaked with 50:50 solution of water and methylated spirits. Larger infestations will require regular spraying with general and systemic insecticides.*
Slugs and snails.	Attracted to young seedlings with soft foliage, emerging flower spikes and flowers. Silvery deposits and trails are left by these slippery pests.	*Slug bait, in the form of pellets, may be scattered on and around the plants.*
Vermin – mice and rats.	Attracted to the warmth of the greenhouse in the winter. These pests clamber up the flower spikes and eat the pollen which is high in protein, also damaging or breaking the spikes.	*Traps and bait. These must be checked regularly.*
Leaf Hopper – small white flies.	These tiny flies accumulate on young foliage, generally on the underside of leaves, where they suck the sap. They are also found on flowers.	*Treat with Malathion.*

DISEASE	CHARACTERISTICS/SYMPTOMS	REMEDY
Damping off, or Basal Rot.	Young seedlings, freshly removed from a flask, are most susceptible to this disease.	*Remove infected plants and drench with fungicide or bactericide. Reduce humidity and watering frequency, and ventilate whenever possible.*
Root Rot	Usually affects newly-potted plants which are watered excessively. Encouraged by general over-watering or poor drainage.	*Re-pot immediately. Reduce the risk of this recurring by careful watering. Remove any dead or decaying roots when repotting.*
Sooty Mould	Black, downy mould found on leaves, which reduces the amount of light and vigour. Often caused by deposits left by greenfly and scale insects.	*Wipe the leaves with cotton wool soaked in a 50:50 solution of water and methylated spirits.*
Viruses	Recognized by yellow or white distinct mottling or streaking on leaves, which may turn black as the foliage ages. Distinct colour breaks in flower which discolour soon after opening. Do not confuse this with insect damage.	*There is no known cure for virus. The plant MUST BE BURNED to eliminate the risk of spreading. Always ensure cutting tools and instruments are sterilized in a flame between uses.*

LEFT: *Phalaenopsis leaves infested with scale insects.*

BELOW: *Paphiopedilum leaves with a mealy bug infestation.*

RIGHT: *Cymbidium leaves showing signs of virus.*

PRESENTATION AND JUDGING

This is one of the most exciting periods in the orchid grower's calendar. The plants which are selected for exhibition should not be restricted to awarded plants or special clones. Any well-flowered orchid will help to create the fine spectacle which the public always expects to see. Beauty is in the eye of the beholder, as they say, and whilst an owner may not see a plant's potential for an award, it may still create great interest and share in the beauty of the show surroundings. It needs to be remembered that any well-grown plant is far better than a highly-awarded variety which has been poorly grown.

The first step is to be able to flower the plants at show time; and secondly, to present them to their best advantage. If you always cultivate your plants with the intention of showing them, you are already part of the way there.

Begin several weeks before the show, by making a selection of the plants which will be ready for the show. If you have a holding bench, and intend moving your plants, ensure that you place them in exactly the same position as they were facing (eg into the light). This will ensure that the buds and flowers do not twist towards the light.

To enhance the colour, green flowers should be placed in a shadier position, while pinks and reds will improve if they are allowed to open in a sunnier aspect. Not all flower spikes will need attention, but those genera which produce tall spikes will require the support of stakes made from bamboo cane or strong wire.

Do not allow flower spikes to die on a plant. Remove them when the first flowers begin to wilt, and enjoy them placed in a vase in water, which if changed regularly, will allow them to last a number of days. If the flowers are left on the plant, it will lose vigour as the ailing spikes will draw excessive nutrients from it.

Cymbidium spikes need to be trained almost as soon as they appear. A cane should be inserted behind the spike. The cane may also serve as a reminder to be cautious when watering, as water can mark and damage the flowers. Once the spike has reached about 1 foot (30 cm) in length, a tie should be applied. Tie the spike securely and firmly, making a figure of eight, with the knot next to the cane. Great care must be taken, as the growing spikes are brittle, and a jolt or rough handling will break them.

When the buds have begun to form, a second tie should be made just below the first bud. You then need to decide whether the spike should arch or stand erect. For arching, an extra cane may be needed; otherwise, extra ties will be needed to keep the spike straight.

ABOVE: *An RHS entry and recommendation (top) and a plant label.*

LEFT: *Display of orchids at the RHS hall, London, 1989.*

BELOW: *McBeans Orchids' display at the 75th Anniversary Chelsea Flower Show, London, 1988.*

FACING PAGE, ABOVE: *McBeans Orchids' display house*

FACING PAGE, CENTRE: *Chelsea Flower Show, 1915.*

FACING PAGE, BELOW: *Charlesworth & Co.'s group of orchids, 1915.*

No more ties than are necessary should be used – a 'trussed' spike does not look elegant.

Odontoglossums may be trained in a similar manner, but they are usually more graceful if allowed to arch. The nature of the spike itself will tend to determine the best method. For example, *Odontoglossum crispum* arches naturally whereas *Odontoglossum bictoniense* produces an upright spike.

Odontoglossum inter-generic hybrids which branch tend to show their flowers better if the terminal spike is erect. Always try to select the thinnest cane or stake for the plant, and snip off any excess string from the knot.

Paphiopedilums differ in that they initially only require staking up to the point where the spike and buds have formed. Place a thin cane behind the stem, which should be tied once on the stem and once below the flower bud. Only when the bud has opened and been allowed to set for five days should the final tie be made, if necessary lifting the angle of the flower.

Miltonias should be allowed to open fully before any cane or support is inserted. When the spike is fully open, insert a cane into the pot and trim it so that the top is halfway down the spike. Splitting the top of the cane will make a fork for the spike to rest on.

Cattleyas should be trained from an early age to grow vertical pseudo-bulbs. When the buds are still in the sheath, a

stake should be inserted behind the flowering pseudo-bulb, and if necessary, a single tie made at its base. A second tie must be made at the point where the bulb and leaf join. Only after the flowers have opened and set should ties be made on the flower stems.

Phalaenopsis hybrids need to be trained upright from when the spikes reach around 8 in (20 cm). A tie should be made under the first bud. These orchids tend to look better if allowed to arch from this point, but additional staking will be necessary to support the spike as the flowers begin to open. If this is not done, the weight of the precious blooms can actually break the spike.

Staking is of the utmost importance when showing flowering plants to their best advantage, and it must be done right from the early stages of spike development. During this time, though, there are a number of other tasks that must be carried out. Check for any pests and diseases, and eradicate them immediately as described in the section on pests and diseases. As a precautionary measure, place a few slug pellets at the base of the spike to kill any slug or snail before it has a chance to damage your flowers. A swab of cotton wool around the base of the spike also discourages these wretched pests.

Cleaning of the foliage must be carried out two or three days before the show, and dead bracts and discoloured leaves removed. Using a sterilized blade, trim any leaf tips which are

damaged to form a natural V-shape. A damp cloth will be needed to clean the leaves, and at this time, especially in the case of Cymbidiums, tie any large leaves away from the flowers.

Clean the pot, removing any unsightly marks or algae. Pot covers or baskets trimmed with moss add to the overall effect. Trim any protruding stakes.

Labelling must be checked. It must be neatly written or typed and contain accurate information. The genus name is followed by the hybrid name or seedling cross and varietal name; then any previous award abbreviations, if applicable.

Entry forms are normally available before the show. Check with the show secretary or manager for any guidance you may require, and complete the forms before your departure.

A good watering is important before the show – the plants may be displayed in air-conditioned premises with low humidity levels.

Before transporting your plants to the show, check to see if they require extra temporary staking. Tissue paper can be placed between the flowers to stop them from rubbing against each other in transit. If the weather is adverse, cover the flowers completely to prevent damage from cold or heat. Do not leave the plants in an unattended vehicle for any length of time en route to the show. On arrival, after seeing the show manager for instructions, carefully remove the tissue paper and extra staking.

Presentation, whether on the show bench or in your home, is always of vital importance. While there seems to be a great deal involved in the lead-up to a show, your tender loving care and efforts will be rewarded. If you see badly presented plants in dirty pots, obviously staked only on the day of the show, with their flowers upside down, you will realize what a difference proper preparation can make.

LEFT: *Tochigi Orchid Growers' Association Best Display.*

FACING PAGE, LEFT: *RHS Award of Merit certificate.*

FACING PAGE, RIGHT: *FCC/ RHS First Class certificate.*

AWARD SYSTEMS AROUND THE WORLD

Award judging involves the close scrutiny of an orchid by qualified judges from one of the many respected international awarding systems around the world. The oldest and most respected is the Royal Horticultural Society's award system, which granted the first award to an orchid in 1859. In the same year, James Veitch & Sons gained the highest and most prestigious award – a First Class Certificate for Cattleya Dormanniana (C. maxima × C. intermedia). The orchids were judged by the Floral Committee of the RHS from 1859 until 1889, when the RHS Orchid Committee was established. The Orchid Committee does not actually grant the awards, but merely recommends them for ratification by the RHS Council. The Orchid Committee also makes recommendations for medal awards for group exhibits which are staged at the RHS Halls throughout the year. A permanent visual record of every awarded plant exists in the form of a painting, a tradition started in 1897.

The RHS Orchid Committee evaluates the plants or cut spikes, without charge to the applicant, using the Appreciation Method. This entails a meeting of a highly authoritative group of orchid judges appointed by the RHS, who discuss each plant entered for award judging. They then vote for the award that has been proposed and seconded, which may be one of the following:

FIRST CLASS CERTIFICATE (FCC/RHS) – *instituted in 1859 for 'orchids of great excellence'.*

CULTURAL COMMENDATION CERTIFICATE (CCC/RHS) – *instituted in 1872. This award is granted to the grower whose exhibit shows 'great cultural skill'.*

AWARD OF MERIT (AM/RHS) – *instituted in 1888 for orchids which are 'meritorious'.*

PRELIMINARY COMMENDATION (PC/RHS) – *instituted in 1931 for 'new orchids of promise'.*

The Appreciation Method offers some leeway in that new breeding trends and breakthroughs may be recognized, whereas a similar orchid may have received a lesser award, or no award at all, under a different judging system.

The Point-scoring System differs in that points are awarded for various criteria. This system is used by the highly-regarded and largest judging institution, the American Orchid Society. Other leading judging authorities around the world also follow this system. All judging systems were established with the primary aim of promoting and recognizing new and superior

forms of orchids. All judges are expected to keep up-
to-date with international breeding trends, and
fairness and neutrality are of utmost importance.
The American system allocates points with at least
30 per cent of the score being granted for the general
form of the flower, the ultimate flower being of full
shape, symmetrical and of closed form. Form is
defined as fullness and roundness, with the segments
arranged equally. A further 30 per cent of the score
is allocated for colour, which should have impact, be
clear and bright and be evenly dispersed without signs
of fading. The remaining 40 per cent is allotted for:

1. Size of flower. This should be equal to or greater
than the geometric average of both parents. The
substance, the gloss or crystalline appearance and
firm texture are also taken into account.

2. Spike habit and/or the arrangement of flowers on
the inflorescence. Bunched and twisted flowers will
lower the marks.

3. The amount of flowers, as applicable to the plant.
An Odontoglossum would be expected to have eight
or more flowers on the spike, while a Paphiopedilum
generally would be accepted with a single bloom.

4. The length of the stem appropriate to the plant.
The final score will be out of a possible 100 points.

American awards include:

First Class Certificate (FCC/AOS) – 90 to 100
points
Award of Merit (AM/AOS) – 80 to 89 points
High Class Certificate (HCC/AOS) – 75 to 79 points
Judges Commendation (JC/AOS)
Award of Quality (AQ/AOS)
Certificate of Horticultural Merit (CHM/AOS)
Certificate of Botanical Rarity (CBR/AOS)
Certificate of Cultural Merit (CCM/AOS)

The permanent record of AOS awarded plants is in
the form of photographic transparencies or slides.
Most judging bodies produce a register of awards in
book form, on a monthly, quarterly or annual basis.
They also provide a handbook outlining the criteria,
the fee and their rules.

There are many awarding bodies throughout the
world. Most work on either the appreciation or the
points system, although some use a combination of
both methods. Some place special emphasis on the
various features of the orchid flower, others on
shape, colour, foliage and so forth.

ORCHID IDENTIFIER

Cymbidiums

Natural genus: Cymbidium
Meaning: (cymbi) kymbe = boat (Greek word referring to the boat-shaped lip)
Origin/habitat: South-east Asia, Himalayas to Japan and China and from the Philippines to New Guinea and Australia
Flowering time: From late summer through to the spring, depending on the parentage of the hybrid
Temperature range: Mostly cool

Cymbidiums have been in cultivation for thousands of years, but hybridizing programmes really only began in the late 1800s and for the miniature types even more recently. Cymbidiums are grown extensively throughout the world both as pot plants and for cut-flower production.

The Cymbidium species are not widely grown, but are being produced by leading orchid nurseries to swell their populations and to reduce further demands on the jungles. *Cymbidium Lowianum* and its various colour forms, *C. tracyanum*, *C. ensifolium*, *C. pumilum*, *C. tigrinum*, *C. Devonianum*, *C. eburneum*, *C. erythrostylum*, *C. grandiflorum* and *C. insigne*, have all been used extensively in the breeding programmes of eminent hybridizers around the world. Each of the above species has been used with specific aims in mind.

FACING PAGE: Cymbidium Angelica's Ultimatum *'Cooksbridge Abundance'* AM/RHS.

RIGHT: Cymbidium tracyanum *'Cooksbridge'*.

BELOW: *A group of* Mini Cymbidium Strathmore Rainbow.

It is the flamboyant hybrids that have attracted collectors and tempted indoor pot plant lovers for many decades. Their popularity is due mostly to the fact that they may be tissue cultured with relative ease. This has resulted in the price of these gorgeous orchids being reduced quite dramatically to an affordable level.

Cymbidiums make superb pot plants, producing flowers that are long-lasting and are available in a full range of colours. With careful selection, a collector should be able to have a collection of varied Cymbidiums which will flower over a six- to nine-month period. Most importantly, given the right conditions, Cymbidiums are the easiest and most rewarding of all orchids.

Cymbidium Western Rose 'Spring Bride' AM/RHS

CYMBIDIUM WESTERN ROSE

'Spring Bride' AM/RHS is the combination of two legendary orchids, *Cym. Alexanderi* 'Westonbirt' FCC/RHS and *C. Vieux Rose* 'Dell Park' FCC/RHS; both of these are tetraploids which have produced fine descendants.

Cymbidium New Dimension 'Mont Millais'

CYMBIDIUM NEW DIMENSION

'Mont Millais' is progeny out of the exquisite *Cym. Mavourneen* 'Jester' and has proved to be an outstanding parent of pastel Miniature Cymbidiums, especially when crossed with *C. putana* to make *Mini Cym. Strathbraan*.

Cymbidium Thurso 'Cooksbridge' AM/RHS

CYMBIDIUM THURSO

'Cooksbridge' AM/RHS (*York Meredith* × *Miretta*) is one of the finest green Cymbidium hybrids ever produced, having superb conformation of shape.

CYMBIDIUM ANGELICA'S ULTIMATUM

'Cooksbridge Abundance' AM/RHS (*Angelica* × *Ultimatum*): the fine shape of this hybrid is derived from the superb grandparent *Cym. Lucy Moor* which has flowers in excess of 5 in (12.5 cm) in diameter.

Cymbidium Goldrun 'Cooksbridge'

CYMBIDIUM GOLDRUN

'Cooksbridge' (*Runnymede* × *Cariga*) is one of the latest non-fading yellow hybrids which will prove its worth with cut-flower growers and collectors alike.

Cymbidium Pontac 'Trinity' AM/RHS

Cymbidium Mavourneen 'Jester' AM/RHS

CYMBIDIUM PONTAC

'Trinity' AM/RHS (*Hamsey* × *Mem. Dr. Borg*) is a fine solid red flower which is highlighted with a soft cream outline. This grex has been highly awarded on the world stage.

CYMBIDIUM MAVOURNEEN

'Jester' AM/RHS (*Miretta* × *Sussex Moor*) is the best example of a peloric Cymbidium which has further proved to be an outstanding parent, having produced progeny of pure colours. Whilst it is only of medium size, its attractive pinky red markings on the petals have made it a real showstopper.

Cymbidium Red Beauty 'Rembrandt' FCC/RHS

Mini Cymbidium Strathdon 'Cooksbridge Noel' AM/RHS

CYMBIDIUM RED BEAUTY

'Rembrandt' FCC/RHS (*Vanguard* × *Tapestry*) is a stunning deep pink flower of exceptional size. This variety is a converted tetraploid and various clones are widely grown in Europe by cut-flower producers because of their distinctive colour, size and lasting qualities.

MINI CYMBIDIUM STRATHDON

'Cooksbridge Noel' AM/RHS (*Nip* × *Kurun*) is the finest early-flowering deep rose pink bloom. It is suitable for Christmas in the Northern hemisphere, and Mother's Day in the Southern. This hybrid has the best characteristics from both parents: the colour from C. *Nip* and the early-flowering qualities from C. *Kurun*

Mini Cymbidium (Lerwick × Precious Pink) 'Lewes Delight'

MINI CYMBIDIUM

'Lewes Delight' (*Lerwick* × *Precious Pink*). This crossing has resulted in very shapely desirable pink flowers which are slightly larger than the usual miniature flowers, being a third generation C. *pumilum* hybrid.

Mini Cymbidium (Lerwick × Marquessa Prescott) 'Lewes Delight'

MINI CYMBIDIUM

'Lewes Delight' (*Lerwick* × *Marquessa Prescott*). This is a super second generation C. *pumilum* (C. *floribunda*) crossing which produced intermediate pink colours.

Mini Cymbidium (Lerwick × Precious Pink) 'Strawberry Blush'

MINI CYMBIDIUM

'Strawberry Blush' (*Lerwick* × *Precious Pink*). Another luscious hybrid with outstanding lip markings, shape and colour.

Mini Cymbidium Gleneagles 'Cooksbridge Supreme'

MINI CYMBIDIUM GLENEAGLES

'Cooksbridge Supreme' (*C. putana* × *C. Precious Pink*). A delightful hybrid which is bred from C. *putana* 'Gem' and which has produced unusual bicoloured flowers.

Mini Cymbidium Lerwick Rose 'Cooksbridge Flamboyance'

MINI CYMBIDIUM LERWICK ROSE

'Cooksbridge Flamboyance' (*C. Lerwick* × *C. Vieux Rose*). Cym. *Vieux Rose* has been responsible for the bicolour characteristics which add so much charm to this grex.

Mini Cymbidium Castle of Mey 'Raspberry Blush'

MINI CYMBIDIUM CASTLE OF MEY

'Raspberry Blush' (*Putana* × *Western Rose*). Many fine clones have been produced from this crossing; from these, more than 15 were selected for meristemming, from a flowering of over one thousand seedlings.

Mini Cymbidium Castle of Mey 'Pinkie' AM/RHS

MINI CYMBIDIUM CASTLE OF MEY

'Pinkie' AM/RHS (*Putana* × *Western Rose*) was certainly the most superb clone to be awarded from this grex. The delicate shell-pink colour has become a new favourite amongst cut-flower growers around the world.

Mini Cymbidium Castle of Mey 'Cooksbridge Jester'

MINI CYMBIDIUM CASTLE OF MEY

'Cooksbridge Jester' AM/RHS (*Putana* × *Western Rose*) was a chance novelty from the large population flowered of this grex.

Mini Cymbidium Mont L'Abbe 'Trinity' AM/RHS

MINI CYMBIDIUM MONT L'ABBE

'Trinity' AM/RHS (*Strathdon* × *Volcano*). In this instance, the C. *Strathdon* was a brown variety and subsequently produced chocolate brown novelty progeny which are fairly uncommon in Cymbidium hybrids.

Mini Cymbidium (Lerwick × Rincon) 'Cooksbridge Supreme'

MINI CYMBIDIUM

'Cooksbridge Supreme' (*Lerwick* × *Rincon*) This hybrid was made with the intention of increasing early-flowering varieties.

Mini Cymbidium Stonehaven 'Cooksbridge'

MINI CYMBIDIUM STONEHAVEN

'Cooksbridge' (C. *putana* × C. *Cariga*). Here the diploid
C. *Cariga* 'Sorrento' was used and produced a fine range of
yellow through to apricot progeny, all of which were desirably
non-fading colours.

*Mini Cymbidium Highland Wood 'Cooksbridge Poly' PC/RHS–
HCC/AOS*

MINI CYMBIDIUM HIGHLAND WOOD

'Cooksbridge Poly' PC/RHS-HCC/AOS (C. *Wood Nymph*
× C. *Western Rose*). This is a very rare second generation
Cym. tigrinum hybrid which also occurs in a range of colours
including lemon yellow, lime-green, pink and bronze-orange
tones.

Mini Cymbidium Latigo 'Cooksbridge Sunset'

MINI CYMBIDIUM LATIGO

'Cooksbridge Sunset' (C. *Dag* × C. *Cariga*). This hybrid is
the result of crossing two colchicine-converted tetraploids to
produce bright orange flowers with a typical banded lip from
C. *Cariga*.

Mini Cymbidium Strathblane 'Lewes'

MINI CYMBIDIUM STRATHBLANE

'Lewes' (C. *Nip* × C. *Remus*). In sharp contrast to many
pastel flowers, this is an eye-catching brick red clone with tall
upright spikes and flowers in the early season.

MINI CYMBIDIUM KINTYRE GOLD

'Cooksbridge Sunny' AM/RHS (C. *putana* ×
C. *Runneymede*). A stunning yellow variety of a new hybrid
which has intermediate sized flowers with very long-lasting
qualities. The flower spikes are very tall and upright, carrying
between 25 and 30 flowers.

Mini Cymbidium Kintyre Gold 'Cooksbridge'

Mini Cymbidium King's Loch 'Lewes'

Mini Cymbidium Strathbraan 'Ice Green'

MINI CYMBIDIUM KINGS LOCH

'Lewes' (*C. King Arthur* × *C. Loch Lomond*). This lime-green hybrid has as a grand-parent the famous American hybrid *C. Sweetheart.* This variety was Best in Class at the 12th World Orchid Conference in Tokyo, 1987.

MINI CYMBIDIUM STRATHBRAAN

(*C. putana* × *C. New Dimension*). Some 15 clones were selected from over 3,000 seedlings which were raised to produce pastel colours. This was achieved, and the colours ranged from pearly white to cream, pastel green and pink, some with heavily marked lips, while others had almost no markings at all.

Mini Cymbidium Strathbraan 'Irish Moss'

Mini Cymbidium Devon Lord 'Viceroy' AM/AOS

Mini Cymbidium Strathbraan 'Ice Maiden'

MINI CYMBIDIUM DEVON LORD

'Viceroy' AM/AOS (*Devon Park* × *Rincon*). This striking orange clone is a third generation *C. Devonianum* hybrid which produces pendulous flower spikes if the plant is grown in a basket, or erect spikes if they are staked. Mid season flowering.

Odontoglossums

Natural genus: Odontoglossum
Meaning: odont = tooth; glossa = tongue (Greek word referring to the projection on the labellum)
Common name: Butterfly orchid
Origin/habitat: Mostly high altitudes of Andes, Guatemala, Mexico, Peru, Colombia, Brazil
Flowering time: Various
Temperature range: Cool to intermediate

Odontoglossum crispum 'Lyoth Demure'

POPULAR ODONTOGLOSSUM INTERGENERIC HYBRIDS	
Alexanderara (Alxra.)	= *Odontoglossum* × *Brassia* × *Cochlioda* × *Oncidium*
Beallara (Bllra.)	= *Odontoglossum* × *Brassia* × *Cochlioda* × *Miltonia*
Burrageara (Burr.)	= *Odontoglossum* × *Cochlioda* × *Miltonia* × *Oncidium*
Colmanara (Colm.)	= *Odontoglossum* × *Miltonia* × *Oncidium*
Degarmoara (Dgmra.)	= *Odontoglossum* × *Brassia* × *Miltonia*
MacLellanara (McLna.)	= *Odontoglossum* × *Brassia* × *Oncidium*
Odontioda (Oda.)	= *Odontoglossum* × *Cochlioda*
Odontobrassia (Odbrs.)	= *Odontoglossum* × *Brassia*
Odontocidium (Odcdm.)	= *Odontoglossum* × *Oncidium*
Odontonia (Odtna.)	= *Odontoglossum* × *Miltonia*
Sanderara (Sand.)	= *Odontoglossum* × *Brassia* × *Cochlioda*
Vuylstekeara (Vuyl.)	= *Odontoglossum* × *Cochlioda* × *Miltonia*
Wilsonara (Wils.)	= *Odontoglossum* × *Cochlioda* × *Oncidium*

The genus Odontoglossum was described by W.H. Alexander Humboldt in 1815 and encompasses some 300 species.

The most popular Odontoglossum species in cultivation are *Odm. crispum*, *O. pescatorei*, *O. rossii*, *O. harryanum*, *O. bictoniense*, *O. uro-skinneri*, *O. pulchellum*, *O. pendulum*, *O. cirrhosum*, *O. cordatum*, *O. grande*, *O. insleyei* and *O. schleperianum*. Many of these are now available through nurseries which have raised them from seed.

Some of the above species have recently been removed from the genus Odontoglossum into genera in their own right, and others into sub-genera. Whilst this is botanically correct, for the purpose of this chapter they have been grouped under the genus Odontoglossum for simplicity, and many collectors still regard them as such.

Odontoglossums are very precise in terms of their cultural requirements. Once these are met, these orchids will thrive and prove that they are, as many have said, the most beautiful of all orchids.

The famous English nursery Charlesworths & Co. have intensively bred many of the finest Odontoglossums over the past hundred years. It is from their breeding programme that the majority of superior hybrids available today are derived. Odontoglossum hybrids occur in almost every colour of the spectrum, in indescribable and bizarre patterns that no kaleidoscope could match.

Odontoglossum crispum 'Lyoth Snowtop' AM/RHS

Odontoglossum crispum 'Golden Gate' AM/AOS

Odontoglossum Royal Occasion 'Lyoth Princess'

ODONTOGLOSSUM CRISPUM

– the most prestigious and famous of all the species – was imported by the boatload prior to and especially at the turn of this century, when fine varieties were known to fetch up to $1,633 (£1,000). O. crispum is in the background of nearly all the modern Odontoglossum alliance hybrids. Probably no other species can boast such intensive line-breeding as *Odm. crispum*; this has been carried out over the past 90 years. O. crispum 'Lyoth Snowtop' AM/RHS is one of the finest forms of this species in cultivation and far superior in form to any newly collected jungle plant.

ODM. PESCATOREI

'Lyoth Delight' is another valuable breeding plant which has laid many a foundation stone in spotted breeding. O. pescatorei 'Lyoth Gem' adds superb shape to its progeny and is behind most of the strongly spotted, blotched and patterned hybrids.

Odontoglossum pescatorei 'Lyoth Delight'

Odontoglossum Durham Pancho 'Lyoth Gold'

ODM. ROYAL OCCASION

(Pancho × Ardentissum) and O. Royal Wedding (Pumistor × Ardentissium) were bred by McBeans and have the albino or xanthotic form of O. crispum in their backgrounds. Both of these hybrids were selected by HRH The Princess of Wales for her wedding bouquet and were named for the occasion in 1981. In the 1920s and 1930s albino Odontoglossums were grown in their thousands by Charlesworths & Co., especially for wedding bouquets. A generation ahead are *Odm. Durham Pancho* 'Lyoth Gold' (Golden Moselle × Pancho) and O. Durham Wedding 'Lyoth Purity' (Royal Wedding × Durham Pancho). These two lovely Odontoglossums were bred on to improve their shape, size and general form, still carrying the albino gene.

Odontioda Golden Rialto 'Lyoth Sunny'

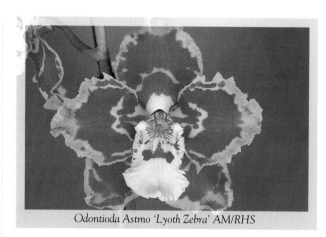

Odontioda Astmo 'Lyoth Zebra' AM/RHS

ODONTIODA GOLDEN RIALTO

'Lyoth Sunny' (*Pacific Gold* × *Rialto*) is a very important hybrid which carries the albino gene. The resultant crossing of *Oda. Rialto* × *Oda. Pacific Gold* produces mostly yellow flowers with brown spotting and an occasional bright yellow albino type.

ODONTIODA ASTMO

'Lyoth Zebra' AM/RHS (*Astliana* × *Moselle*). This was a breakthrough in the breeding of this colour type, having large well shaped flowers of heavy substance.

Odontioda Gold Moselle 'Lyoth Sunshine' AM/RHS

ODONTIODA GOLDEN MOSELLE

'Lyoth Sunshine' AM/RHS (*Pacific Gold* × *Moselle*) was a breakthrough in the production of high quality yellow flowers.

ODONTOGLOSSUM BUTTERCRISP

(*Brimstone Butterfly* × *Crispiana*) is an excellent parent producing large flowers which are inherited from the *Odm. crispum* line of breeding.

Odontoglossum Buttercrisp 'Lyoth Sunburst'

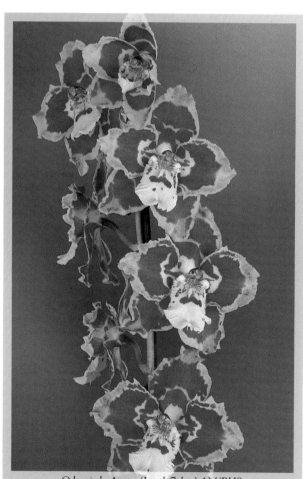

Odontioda Astmo 'Lyoth Zebra' AM/RHS

Odontioda Petit Port 'Lyoth Fantastique'

ODONTIODA PETIT PORT

'Lyoth Fantastique' (*Margia* × *Colwell*) is, as its name implies, ä simply superb, almost flawless flower of great colour and character.

Odontioda Lynx 'Lyoth Apollo'

ODONTIODA LYNX

'Lyoth Apollo' (*Astliana* × *Cadmium*) began a major new line of breeding of yellow-based flowers with patterning.

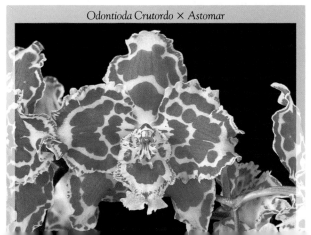

Odontioda Crutordo × Astomar

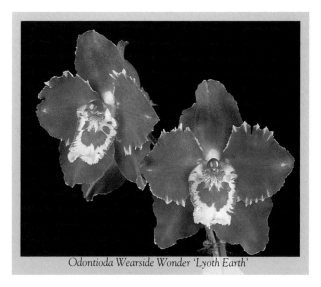

Odontioda Wearside Wonder 'Lyoth Earth'

The sandy colours of *Oda. Wearside Wonder* 'Lyoth Earth' (*Ingmar* × *Corning*) are uncommon and sought after within this group.

Odontioda St. Clement 'Lyoth Rotunda'

ODONTIODA ST CLEMENT

'Lyoth Rotunda' (*Elpheon* × *Crutordo*) is from the finest Odontioda crossing ever made. It is the most highly-awarded Odontioda, and in 1988 was named Orchid of the Year in New Zealand.

ODONTIODA

(*Crutordo* × *Astomar*) has a common parent with *Oda. St Clement*, which is responsible for the intrinsic markings, shape and size.

Odontioda Heatonensis 'Lyoth Petite'

ODONTIODA HEATONENSIS

(*Oda. sanguinea* × *cirrhosum*) is a primary hybrid bred in 1906 by Charlesworths & Co., which is miniature in growth and flower size. *Oda. cirrhosum* has handed on the distinctive shape of the flowers, which *Oda. Heatonensis* continues to pass on to its progeny.

Odontoglossum Pumistor 'Lyoth Giant'

ODONTOGLOSSUM PUMISTOR

'Lyoth Giant' (*Cristor* × *crispum*) is a very fine example of an *Odm. crispum*-type hybrid which was registered in 1969 and is still used for breeding today.

Odontioda Matanda 'Lyoth Gentian'

ODONTIODA MATANDA

'Lyoth Gentian' (*Matrona* × *Pumanda*) was a breakthrough in the production of lavender, blue and mauve tones. This plant is a fine breeder in continuing these lines of colour.

Odontoglossum Incaspum 'Lyoth Splash'

ODONTOGLOSSUM INCASPUM

'Lyoth Splash' (*Crispum* × *Incana*). This hybrid's markings indicate that *Odm. pescatorei* has been used several times in its parentage.

ODONTIODA DURHAM DESTINY

'Lyoth Tyne' AM/RHS (*Flocalo* × *Tusonia*). *Oda. Flocalo* has produced a range of delicate hues, often with picot edging.

Odontioda (Heatonensis × *Ingmar)*

ODONTIODA

(*Heatonensis* × *Ingmar*): when *Oda. Heatonensis* is crossed on to a fine red Odontoglossum, the shape is improved, but the miniature characteristics of the flowers still maintain their charm.

Odontioda Durham Destiny 'Lyoth Tyne' AM/RHS

Odontioda Harrods Forever 'Lyoth Delight' PC/RHS

ODONTIODA HARRODS FOREVER

'Lyoth Delight' PC/RHS (*Stropheon* × *Matanda*) was named in honour of the famous London store. To date, there have been several awarded varieties, varying in colour from almost white through to pink and lilac – all have been of impeccable quality.

The intense glow of luminous colours is typified by the cross *Oda. Ingmar* 'Lyoth Royal' (*Ingera* × *Mardley*). This variety is a remarkable and reliable breeder, producing progeny of similar colours.

Odontioda Durham Castle 'Lyoth Ruby'

ODONTIODA DURHAM CASTLE

'Lyoth Ruby' (*Trixon* × *Ingmar*). This crossing is the latest Odontioda to have received a First Class Certificate from the Royal Horticultural Society. The entire cross has tended to be solid reds and of excellent full shapes. This crossing is the result that hybridists have aimed for for many years and may be termed a 'red *Odm. crispum*'.

Odontioda Ingmar 'Lyoth Royal'

Oncidium tigrinum × *Odontioda Moselle*

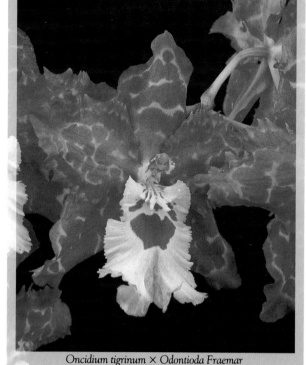

Oncidium tigrinum × Odontioda Fraemar

ODONTOCIDIUM

(*Onc. tigrinum* × *Oda. Moselle*): with the introduction of the Oncidium, this type of Odontoglossum intergeneric hybrid has proved to be slightly more warmth-tolerant than pure Odontoglossum or Odontioda hybrids. A mature plant will produce tall upright flower scapes with numerous flowers, very often on a branched inflorescence.

Another combination using *Oncidium tigrinum*, *Wilsonara Marvidia* (*Onc. tigrinum* × *Oda. Fremar*) has indicated the importance of this species as a parent creating attractive large, broad lips.

Wilsonara Golden Moselle

WILSONARA GOLD MOSELLE

(*Sussex Gold* × *Odm. Moselle*) has another interesting Oncidium species in its background. This time *Onc. sphacelatum* has been introduced two generations back with the aim of reducing the flower size but intensifying the colour and increasing the number of blooms. With the influence of the Oncidium, the progeny have become more warmth-tolerant than pure Odontoglossums.

Paphiopedilums

Natural genus: Paphiopedilum
Meaning: Paphia = Goddess Venus, pedilon = slipper or shoe
The meaning is derived from the Greek words which refer to the pouch
Common name: Lady Slipper or Slipper orchid
Origin/habitat: South-east Asia, Philippines, Malaysia, New Guinea and China
Flowering time: Late autumn to early spring
Temperature range: Intermediate to warm

Paphiopedilums have been favoured by collectors since the mid 1800s and have for many decades been considered by many to be the connoisseur's orchid. The reason for this is that Paphiopedilums can only be multiplied by seed or division; therefore the number of superior varieties available are considerably fewer than those of other genera. The first Cypripedium hybrid (as they were known then) was registered by Veith, in England in 1869. It was named *Cypripedium Harrisianum* (*barbatum* × *villosum*) and was awarded an FCC/RHS in 1869. Paphiopedilums make super house plants with their flowers being so long lasting. Slipper orchids are also used extensively for cut flowers, especially in Europe.

Due to all the recent changes restricting the international movement of Paphiopedilum species, it has become more and more difficult to obtain them. However, there are a number of legitimate orchid breeders who have through the decades collected fine specimens and have begun to raise Paphiopedilum species from seed. All Paphiopedilum species are highly sought after, with the main interest groups being

● the Brachypetalum section which includes *Paphiopedilum bellatulum*, *P. concolor*, *P. niveum* and *P. godefroyae*.
● the Barbata section which encompasses *Paphiopedilum callosum*, *P. barbatum*, *P. lawrenceanum* and *P. argus*.
● the Cochlopetalum group: *Paphiopedilum chamberlainianum*, *P. glaucophyllum* and *P. primulinum*.
● the Mastigopetalum group which includes the regal *Paphiopedilum Rothschildianum*, the controversial *P. Sanderianum*, *P. philippinense* and *P. stonei*.
● the Parvisepalum group which includes the newly discovered species *Paphiopedilum armeniacum*, *P. micranthum*, *P. malipoense* and *P. emmersonii*.

These groups are by no means complete, but cover the most popular species which are regularly used in hybridizing. Obviously the most recent discoveries have only just been introduced and the Paphiopedilum fraternity are waiting in anticipation for the new hybrids to flower in quantity.

PAPHIOPEDILUM BELLATULUM

'Red Fusion' B/CSA is the outstanding and exciting result of a recent sibling cross. *P. bellatulum* has been used extensively in hybridizing to enhance the shape of the progeny.

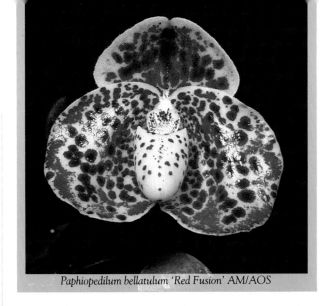

Paphiopedilum bellatulum 'Red Fusion' AM/AOS

Paphiopedilum callosum var. Sanderae 'Blaze'

PAPHIOPEDILUM CALLOSUM

var. Sanderae 'Blaze' is the albino form of the usually pink and white species. This species has marbled foliage which, even when out of flower, is extremely attractive. *P. callosum* was until recently found only in two colour forms, the rose pink coloratum form and the albino or white and green form, but a very dark variety was discovered which has led to increased popularity of late. The dark maroon or vinicoloured variety has been used to remake many of the early primary hybrids.

PAPHIOPEDILUM LAWRENCEANUM

var. *Hyeanum* is another albino form of this species and it also occurs naturally in a coloratum or pink form.

Paphiopedilum Lawrenceanum var. hyeanum

PAPHIOPEDILUM MAUDIAE

'Magnificum' FCC/RHS is the result of a crossing of the above two species. The famous *P. Maudiae* was made by Charlesworths & Co. in 1900 and received its award in 1901. This cross is still a highly desirable primary hybrid and still receiving awards. The renowned pink cultivar is variety coloratum and more recently the wine-red, vinicolour types have been produced. Nowadays plants of this type of breeding are often referred to as *Paphiopedilum Maudiae*-type hybrids.

Paphiopedilum Maudiae Vinicolor

PAPHIOPEDILUM MAUDIAE

'Barcombe Burgundy' is the result of a sibling cross of two selected *P. Maudiae* clones. In this instance *P. Maudiae* var. *coloratum* 'Wyld Court' was crossed with *P. Maudiae* var. *vinicolour* 'Tilgates' AM/RHS.

Paphiopedilum Via Quatal 'Blaze'

Paphiopedilum Masupi 'Chailey' PC/RHS

PAPHIOPEDILUM VIA QUATAL

'Blaze' (*Maudiae* × *William Matthews*). This hybrid is typical of Maudiae-type line breeding, with the ultimate aim of gradually producing bigger and better types.

PAPHIOPEDILUM MASUPI

'Chailey' PC/RHS (*Maudiae* × *Supersuk*). Here the vinicolour *P. Maudiae* has been combined with a *P. sukhakulii* hybrid with splendid results.

Paphiopedilum sukhakulii

Paphiopedilum (Clarissa × Vintner's Treasure) 'Boysenberry'

PAPHIOPEDILUM SUKHAKULII

'Blaze' is a good example of this fine species which has the distinctive spotted petals.

PAPHIOPEDILUM RAISIN PIE

'Cooksbridge' (*sukhakulii* × *Clarissa*). The characteristic spotting from *P. sukhakulii* is dominant in nearly all of its progeny. *P. Clarissa* has been used in this instance to increase the overall size of all segments.

PAPHIOPEDILUM RAVEN

'Boysenberry' (*Clarissa* × *Vintner's Treasure*). In this hybrid a coloratum type has been crossed with a vinicolour for best results.

PAPHIOPEDILUM MEM. ROBERT WARD

'Blaze' (*Maudiae* × *Watercolor Artist*). In this crossing a first generation *P. mastersianum* hybrid has been introduced to add green, orange and brown tones.

Paphiopedilum Raisin Pie 'Cooksbridge'

Paphiopedilum Mem. Robert Ward 'Blaze'

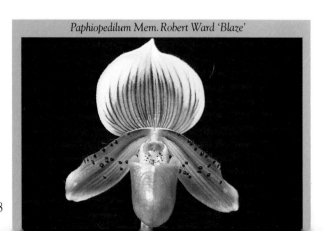

Paphiopedilum urbanianum 'Noelle' AM/AOS

PAPHIOPEDILUM URBANIANUM
'Noelle' AM/AOS. This fairly recent discovery originates from the Philippines and was named in honour of Mrs Jacinta Urban whose family have been involved with orchids in Quezon City in Manila for many generations. This variety is a superb example of this species.

Paphiopedilum concolor

PAPHIOPEDILUM CONCOLOR
'Butterball' is a charming compact species which is easily grown in free-draining composts.

PAPHIOPEDILUM WILLIAM FOGARTY
'Banana Boat' (*Wellesleyanum × sukhakulii*)
P. Wellesleyanum is a hybrid bred from *P. concolor* and has combined its charm with the delightful spotting from *P. sukhakulii*.

Paphiopedilum William Fogarty 'Banana Boat'

Paphiopedilum malipoense 'Mik Mak'

PAPHIOPEDILUM MALIPOENSE
'Mik Mak' is one of the stunning new discoveries from China. A surprising characteristic of this species is the delicious aroma of raspberries which it exudes from the enlarged pouch.

Paphiopedilum armeniacum 'Bramley' AM/RHS

PAPHIOPEDILUM ARMENIACUM
'Bramley' AM/RHS is a recently awarded variety of yet another new find. The golden yellow colour and subtle fragrance never ceases to amaze collectors who patiently await the progeny to be flowered from the many hybrids which have been made.

Paphiopedilum Lord Derby 'The King' FCC/RHS

PAPHIOPEDILUM LORD DERBY

'The King' FCC/RHS (*Rothschildianum × superbiens*) (syn. *Paph. W. R. Lee*) is a fine example of a multifloral Paphiopedilum hybrid, even though it was bred towards the end of the last century.

Paphiopedilum (Bengal Lancers × Rothschildianum)

PAPHIOPEDILUM

(*Bengal Lancers × Rothschildianum*) This is a combination of three multifloral species all adding their superb characteristics to this seedling.

Paphiopedilum sanderianum 'Winfield'

PAPHIOPEDILUM SANDERIANUM

This species was extensively featured at the turn of the century and the most prestigious hybrid, *Paphiopedilum Prince Edward of York* (*Sanderianum × Rothschildianum*) is recorded in print in the Royal Botanic Garden, Kew Herbarium, UK. However, the species was thought to be extinct and lost from cultivation until recent jungle pickers found this species at new locations. *P. Sanderianum* is characterized by its ribbon-like petals which are 18–30 inches (45–60 cm) in length.

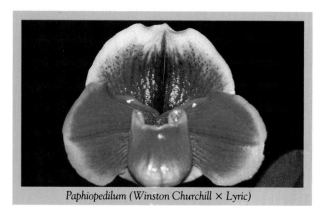

Paphiopedilum (Winston Churchill × Lyric)

PAPHIOPEDILUM

(*Winston Churchill × Lyric*). Both parents have contributed to the intense red colour of this complex hybrid.

PAPHIOPEDILUM BROWNSTONE

'Cooksbridge' (*Hazella × Beedon*) is the finest seedling from this grex, typifying the exceptional qualities of both its parents.

Paphiopedilum Brownstone 'Cooksbridge'

Paphiopedilum Buckhurst 'Mont Millais' AM/RHS

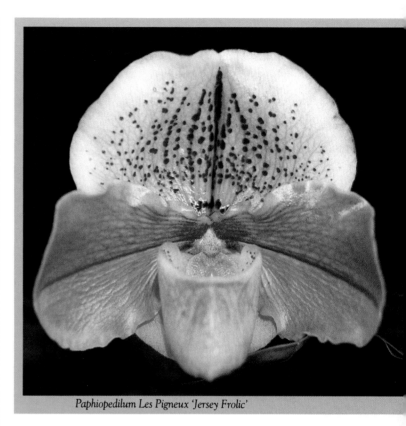

Paphiopedilum Les Pigneux 'Jersey Frolic'

PAPHIOPEDILUM BUCKHURST

'Mont Millais' AM/RHS (*Spring Vigil × Greenville*) has proved to be a super parent, offering superb features of full shape and size to its progeny.

PAPHIOPEDILUM LES PIGNEAUX

'Jersey Frolic' (*Greenstede × World Frolic*). Here the parent *P. Greenstede* diluted the large spots of the *P. World Frolic* into speckles.

Paphiopedilum (Rod McLellan × Gaymaid) 'Jersey Ice'

Paphiopedilum (Milmoore × Bagley)

PAPHIOPEDILUM

'Jersey Ice' (*Rod McLellan × Gaymaid*). This is the result of crossing two superb green Paphiopedilums together.

PAPHIOPEDILUM

(*Milmoore × Bagley*). Two spotted Paphiopedilums were crossed with the intention of enhancing the chestnut brown petals and pouch which contrast with the clean dorsal.

Cattleyas

Natural genus: Cattleya
Meaning: This genus was named by the famous botanist John Lindley after Mr John Cattley
Origin/habitat: Central America, Brazil, Mexico, Colombia and Guatemala
Flowering time: Generally late autumn through to early spring
Temperature range: Intermediate to warm

POPULAR CATTLEYA INTERGENERIC HYBRIDS

Brassocattleya (Bc.)	= Cattleya × Brassavola
Brassolaeliocattleya (Blc.)	= Cattleya × Brassavola × Laella
Cattleytonia (Ctna.)	= Cattleya × Broughtonia
Hawkinsara (Hknsa)	= Cattleya × Broughtonia × Laelia × Sophronitis
Laeliocattleya (Lc.)	= Cattleya × Laelia
Potinara (Pot.)	= Cattleya × Brassavola × Laelia × Sophronitis
Sophrocattleya (Sc.)	= Cattleya × Sophronitis
Sophrolaeliocattleya (Slc.)	= Cattleya × Laelia × Sophronitis

Cattleya Skinneri var. alba

Many Cattleya alliance species have been line-bred with excellent results in recent years and the most desirable of these have been propagated by tissue culture in commercial nurseries. This has made them more accessible to collectors, removing the need to draw on the jungle resources which are dwindling.

Cattleya aurantiarca, *C. Aclandiae*, *C. amethystoglossa*, *C. Bowringiana*, *C. Dowiana*, *C. guttata*, *C. intermedia*, *C. Loddegesii*, *C. Leuddemaniana*, *C. Percivaliana* and *C. Skinneri* are amongst the most popular species in cultivation. Their various colour forms have attracted growers' attention.

Most of the modern hybridizing is carried out by leading nurseries in America and particularly Hawaii.

Since shipments of orchids began to arrive in England, it was the Cattleya alliance which attracted much attention when the first one flowered in the collection of Mr John Cattley in the 1820s, because of the intense perfume, bright colour and sheer size of the blooms.

The flowers of *Cattleya labiata* stunned horticultural circles when the large rose pink flower with its deep crimson-purple lip opened. From then on, large consignments were imported by the boat load.

The Sander's List of Orchid Hybrids lists more Cattleya alliance and inter-generic hybrids than any other genus. This is primarily because of the complexity of this group of orchids which may be hybridized quite freely.

Cattleyas have seen a continual increase in their popularity as new hybrids are created, through miniaturization and new inter-generic groups.

The Cattleya species are widely grown by collectors but are not used to any great degree by commercial growers of cut-flower varieties. It will be the showier hybrids that will be cultivated for this use.

Cattleya dowiana var. aurea

CATTLEYA DOWIANA
var. *aurea* is a bright and showy species which is extensively grown in cultivation and has been responsible for much of the yellow and bicoloured Cattleya breeding.

Cattleya Leuddemanniana

Cattleya (Candytuft × Angelwalker)

CATTLEYA LEUDDEMANNIANA
is behind many of the large pink Cattleya hybrids which are still very sought after. Its superbly rich amethyst, yellow and white lip character has caught the eye of many a newcomer to the field.

CATTLEYA
(*Candytuft* × *Angelwalker*). This delicate pink hybrid has been dominated by miniature *Cattleya walkeriana*, itself a delightful species.

Laelia anceps var. Veitchiana

Laeliocattleya Susan Holguin

LAELIA ANCEPS
var. *Veitchiana* is an easy to grow natural species which occurs in as many as 14 known colour forms.

LAELIOCATTLEYA SUSAN HOLGUIN
(*Jose Dias Castro* × *C.J.A. Carbone*). This is a superb example of a standard, full-shaped Cattleya alliance hybrid packed with character.

Cattleya Jungle Spots

CATTLEYA JUNGLE SPOTS

'Blumen Insel' (*Fascelis* × *oclandiae*): in sharp contrast to full, shapely flowers, this primary hybrid has tremendous impact with the boldly spotted segments and shocking pink spade lip.

Brassolaeliocattleya Golden Jubilee

BRASSOLAELIOCATTLEYA GOLDEN JUBILEE

(*Waikiki Gold* × *Bouton D'Or*). The striking golden yellow flowers of this clone are typical of both parents. *Blc. Bouton D'Or* hybrids have become more popular recently both for the reasons mentioned above and for their willingness to flower.

Brassolaeliocattleya Rangers Six 'A OK'

BRASSOLAELIOCATTLEYA RANGER SIX

'A–OK' (*Nacouchee* × *C. Empress Bells*). This stunning white hybrid has inherited from *C. Empress Bells* the fine standards of white Cattleya alliance breeding. The albino forms of *Cattleya trianae*, *C. mossiae* and *C. gaskelliana* are striking in this lovely orchid.

Laeliocattleya Petticoats 'Blumen Insel'

LAELIOCATTLEYA PETTICOATS

'Blumen Insel' (*Pirate King* × *Colorama*) is a splash petal or peloric Cattleya hybrid. This characteristic is the result of using *C. intermedia* var. *acquinii*, a great-grandparent of this tricoloured orchid.

Sophrolaeliocattleya Jewelers Art

SOPHROLAELIOCATTLEYA JEWELER'S ART

(*Lc. Drumbeat* × *Sc. Doris*) takes its colour inheritance from *Sophrocattleya Doris*, which is the interesting combination of the miniature red *Sophronitis coccinea* and the delightful *Cattleya dowiana* var. *aurea* which, in turn, is crossed onto a large-flowered Cattleya hybrid.

Sophrolaeliocattleya Dixie Jewels 'Suzuki' FCC/AOS

Sophrolaeliocattleya Mine Gold

SOPHROLAELIOCATTLEYA DIXIE JEWELS

'Suzuki' FCC/AOS (*Madge Fordyce* × *Aclandiae*). The astounding solid red flowers have the superb substance and glistening texture which make this hybrid so superior; the plant has retained its miniature status.

SOPHROLAELIOCATTLEYA MINE GOLD

'Lump o'Gold' (*L. briegeri* × *Jewel Box*). *L. briegeri* has been responsible for increasing the length of the stem and miniaturizing the growth habit. Its association with *C. aurantica* has maintained the number of flowers and colour intensity. Being small and compact in stature, this type of Cattleya alliance hybrid has gained enormous popularity of late.

Sophrolaeliocattleya Hazel Boyd 'Splash'

Cattleytonia Why Not

SOPHROLAELIOCATTLEYA HAZEL BOYD

'Splash' (*California Apricot* × *Jewel Box*). Probably no other miniature Cattleya has been so highly awarded. Its colours range from yellows through to apricots, pinks and scarlet reds. *Sophronitis coccinea* and *Cattleya aurantica* feature in the ancestry of these fine minatures.

CATTLEYTONIA WHY NOT

(*C. aurantiarca* × *Bro. sanguinea*). A fairly new innovation and another miniature hybrid. In this instance the stem length is increased by using the Jamaican species *Broughtonia sanguinea* which is also characterized by clustered bunches of flowers.

Miltonias

Natural genus: Miltonia
Meaning: Named in honour of Viscount Milton
Common name: Pansy orchid
Origin/habitat: Miltonias are widespread at various altitudes throughout Central America
Flowering time: Various
Temperature range: Intermediate to warm

Miltonias were imported into Europe during the latter years of the 18th century, with M. *vexillaira* being much in demand for its delightful natural sprays of flowers. By the early 1900s leading suppliers of orchids were offering no less than 26 different varieties of *Miltonia vexillaira*. Many cultivars received First Class Certificates from the RHS before the turn of the century. Of all early Miltonia hybrids M. *Charlesworthii* is most significant; registered in 1912, this charming hybrid is still used for breeding today.

Exhibitors at the early Chelsea Flower Shows displayed hundreds of these dainty gems in banked groups typical of exhibits from that era.

It was not until the late 1960s that Miltonia hybridizing programmes began again; since then there has been another resurgence in their popularity in the late 1980s. The often slightly fragrant Pansy orchid has now been fully accepted as a houseplant of the future as more and more of the public have found their cultivation to be fairly simple.

Nearly all the species are widely grown in cultivation with the more sought after being *Miltonia Bluntii*, M. *Clowesii*, M. *flavescens*, M. *phalaenopsis*, M. *Roezlii*, M. *spectabilis* and M. *vexillaira* and their various colour forms.

Numerous hybrids now exist with prolific parents being *Miltonia Hamburg*, M. *Hanover*, M. *Memoria Ida Seigal*, M. *Red Knight*, M. *Emotion*, M. *Lingwood* and M. *Edwidge Sabourin*.

Miltonias are always greatly admired when grouped en masse in natural settings. Given the correct climatic conditions and plenty of humidity, Miltonias will quickly multiply into specimen plants.

Miltonia specimen

MILTONIA SPECTABILIS
var. *Moreliana* 'Cooksbridge Plum'. One of the warmer growing species which naturally occurs in Brazil. This is an exceptionally fine clone of this species being of deeper colour and having larger flowers than usual.

Miltonia 'Hamburg'

Miltonia vexillaria 'Arctic Moon'

MILTONIA VEXILLAIRA
'Arctic Moon' AM/AOS is an attractive cultivar of a species which has been in cultivation for over 100 years and is still being used in modern breeding programmes.

Miltonia Violet 'Tears'

MILTONIA VIOLET

'Tears' (*Lypatia* × *Lingwood*). Instead of the blotched mask, M. *Violet* shows the delicate waterfall pattern which has become synonymous with many showy Miltonia hybrids.

Miltonia Brutips

MILTONIA BRUTIPS

(*Bremen* × *Lilac Time*). The intense waterfall markings have originated in this instance from M. *Violet* which is a parent of M. *Lilac Time*. This clone is quite remarkable; whilst not producing many flowers per spike, it will produce up to four or five spikes per bulb.

Miltonia Charlesworthii 'Raphael'

Miltonia Lyceana

MILTONIA CHARLESWORTHII

'Raphael' (*vexillaira* × *Roezlii*) is a stunning white which is offset by the black central mask, which it passes on to its progeny. M. *Charlesworthii* also occurs in shades of white, cream and pastel pink.

MILTONIA LYCEANA

(*Lord Lambourne* × *Princess Margaret*). This combination resulted in the production of outstanding white flowers which have cherry red blushing on the segments and a bright yellow mask in the centre.

Miltonia Lambton Castle 'Cooksbridge' AM/RHS

MILTONIA LAMBTON CASTLE
'Cooksbridge' AM/RHS (*Franz Wichman × Irma*), awarded in 1986, has shapely, colourful and desirably flat deep pink flowers.

Miltonia phalaenopsis 'Ardingly'

MILTONIA PHALAENOPSIS
'Ardingly' from Colombia is closely allied to the Odontoglossum genus. Its delightfully whimsical flowers have added a delicate touch to its progeny.

Miltonia Blueana 'Reine Elizabeth' (vexillaira × Roezlii)

MILTONIA BLUEANA
'Reine Elizabeth' (*vexillaira × Roezlii*) was registered in 1889 but is still in existence in collections today. It was one of the first Miltonia hybrids to also be successfully crossed with the Odontoglossum alliance.

Miltonia Hyeana (Blueana × vexillaira)

MILTONIA HYEANA
(*Blueana × vexillaira*). Another relic from the past but quite significant in the line breeding of more shapely Miltonia hybrids.

Miltonia Gattonense 'Albana'

MILTONIA GATTONENSE

'Albans' (*Blueana* × *Jules Hye de Crom*) indicates the vast strides which have been achieved in producing fine progeny. M. *Gattonense* is itself an almost pure line-bred M. *vexillaira*.

Miltonia Robert Strauss 'Ardingly' AM/RHS

MILTONIA ROBERT STRAUSS

'Ardingly' AM/RHS (*Gattonense* × *Augusta*). The large flat labellum characteristic of M. *Gattonense* has dominated in this crossing. Within the grex the colours have generally been whites and creams with attractive central maskings. M. *Augusta* is also a line-bred M. *vexillaira*.

Phalaenopsis

Natural genus: Phalaenopsis
Meaning: phalaenia = moth (Greek); opsis = resemblance (referring to the flowers)
Common name: Moth orchid
Origin/habitat: Far East, tropical Asia, Malaysia, Philippines
Flowering time: Various
Temperature: Tropical

POPULAR PHALAENOPSIS INTERGENERIC HYBRIDS

Asconopsis (Ascps.)	= *Phalaenopsis* × *Ascocentrum*
Devereuxara (Dvra.)	= *Phalaenopsis* × *Ascocentrum* × *Vanda*
Doritaenopsis (Dtps.)	= *Phalaenopsis* × *Doritis*
Ernestara (Entra.)	= *Phalaenopsis* × *Renanthera* × *Vandopsis*
Renanthopsis (Rnthps.)	= *Phalaenopsis* × *Renanthera*
Sarconopsis (Srnps.)	= *Phalaenopsis* × *Sarcochilus*
Vandaenopsis (Vdnps.)	= *Phalaenopsis* × *Vanda*

The genus Phalaenopsis encompasses some 70 extremely interesting and very variable species. Whilst they demand plenty of heat and moisture to grow successfully they are undeniably value for money, with the flowers often lasting for months at a time. It is the lasting qualities, the range of colours and their intrinsic beauty that has given rise to their success in recent years.

It is also notable that when most of the flowers have fallen from the spike it may be cut down to approximately one inch (2.5 cm) above the second node from the base and in many cases a secondary flower spike will emerge. After the second flowering the spike should be removed close to the base of the plant. This will allow the plant to concentrate its efforts on vegetative growth, which is necessary for the well-being of the plant. Hybridization has been carried out extensively worldwide within this genus and some notable intergeneric hybrids have also been made with the introduction of Renanthera, Doritis, Vanda and Ascocenda, to name a few.

To date, thousands of Phalaenopsis hybrids have been registered, with new bi-coloured and peloric innovations and novelty type breeding being in demand.

White Phalaenopsis breeding may have reached its peak but breeders are continually improving the standards of this niche with shape and flower count of these stunning flowers which are heavily in demand by florists. The decorative value of a well flowered Phalaenopsis spike is unrivalled: the floriferous habit requires few (if any) additional flowers to create a wonderful bouquet. Pastel and solid deep pink colours are also in demand.

Early jungle collectors must have been struck with awe when initially confronted by the shimmering pendulous spikes of Phalaenopsis which, as the name implies, resemble moths in flight. For some of these jungle beauties not only have incredibly beautiful flowers but also have silver patterned leaves. Their flowers vary in colour and size from large bold whites through to miniature striped and solid and pastel hues.

Nursery raised species are becoming more accessible with intensive work being carried out by nurseries with species conservation in mind. More and more catalogues are offering these and the listings are continually growing with *Phalaenopss amabilis*, *P. cornu-cervi*, *P. equestris*, various varieties of *P. Leuddemanniana*, *P. Leuchorroda*, *P. schilleriana*, *P. stuartiana*, *P. mariae* and three forms of *P. violacea* being the most popular.

Phalaenopsis Amabilis

PHALAENOPSIS AMABILIS
is the species behind the large white standard type Phalaenopsis which are so much in demand by flower trade for their naturally cascading white flowers.

Phalaenopsis Sussex Pearl

PHALAENOPSIS SUSSEX PEARL
'Southern Opera' (*Lady Alice* × *Barclays Celebration*). This white hybrid has sizeable flowers of superb shape and substance and has been known to produce a spike which carried 27 first class flowers.

Phalaenopsis stuartiana

PHALAENOPSIS STUARTIANA
from the Philippines has been used extensively as a parent in order to increase the number of flowers per spike, in addition to branching the spike habit. The modern spotted hybrids have this delightful species in their background.

Phalaenopsis Joseph Hampton

PHALAENOPSIS JOSEPH HAMPTON
'Southern Snowflake' (*Monarch Gem* × *Doris*) is simply one of the finest white Moth orchids ever produced and has successfully been used many times as a parent of equally good progeny. Its parent *P. Doris* is one of the most famous stepping stones in this line of breeding, which itself is a result of line bred *P. amabilis*.

Phalaenopsis Fifi 'Katja'

PHALAENOPSIS FIFI

'Katja' (*Minouche × Redfan*). The delightful apricot lip colouring never ceases to tempt, even though the flowers lack a perfect shape.

Phalaenopsis Barclays Celebration

PHALAENOPSIS BARCLAYS CELEBRATION

'Lewes Jubilee' (*Champagne Lady × Aubaine*). Both parents are used for cut flower production and have been crossed in order to produce a new generation of whites.

Phalaenopsis Sussex Scenario

PHALAENOPSIS SUSSEX SCENARIO

'Southern Duet' (*Sussex Melody × Eva Lou*). In order to increase the size of the bi-coloured P. *Eva Lou* and intensify the light pink lip of P. *Sussex Melody*, this crossing was made. The contrasting colours of this type of breeding have influenced their growing popularity.

PHALAENOPSIS SPACE QUEEN

'Southern Gal' (*Barbara Moler × Temple Cloud*). While P. *Barbara Moler* was registered in 1971 and may be considered as 'passe' by some hybridists, there is still a constant stream of tremendous hybrids being produced, of which P. *Space Queen* is no exception. These plants have proved to be extremely free-flowering and produce elegant spikes often carrying up to 12 and 15 lovely flowers.

Phalaenopsis (Lady Ruby × Redfan)

PHALAENOPSIS

'Southern Ruby' (*Lady Ruby × Redfan*). Here two bi-coloured (white with deep pink lip) Phalaenopsis have been combined to improve the intensity of the coloured lip.

Phalaenopsis Space Queen

Doritaenopsis (stuarto-schilleriana × Happy Valentine)

DORITAENOPSIS

(*Happy Valentine* × *P. stuart-schilleriana*). *Dtps. Happy Valentine* is an exceptionally fine, full shaped flower which in this instance has been crossed with a floriferous primary hybrid. While the size has been reduced somewhat, the shape has been dramatically improved, as has the number of flowers on the scape.

Phalaenopsis Cashmore 'Banana Shake'

PHALAENOPSIS CASHMORE

'Banana Shake' (*Barbara Moler* × *Party Dress*). A large population was flowered from this crossing and it produced small to medium shapely blooms from whites and creams to yellows, apricots and pastel pinks. All the flowers were delicately speckled with various degrees of pink spotting.

Phalaenopsis Lippeglut × dtps. Marta di Rivella

DORITAENOPSIS

(*Marta di Rivalla* × *P. Lippeglut*). The combination of these two superior orchids must surely delight even the most distinguished collectors of quality Phalaenopsis.

Phalaenopsis Barbara Buddah

PHALAENOPSIS BARBARA BUDDAH

'Golden Glow' (*Barbara Moler* × *Golden Buddah*). The influence of P. Spica (*fascito* × *lueddamanniana*) is doubled up in this hybrid occurring in both parents; as expected, the hybrid has taken on the combined appearance of the species.

Phalaenopsis (Dorset Bride × chamade)

PHALAENOPSIS

(*Dorset Bride* × *Chamade*) 'Candy Swirls' owes much of its character to *P. Lady Ruby* which is dominant in producing candy striping and deep coloured lip markings.

Phalaenopsis (Ella Freed × stuartiana) 'Harlequin'

Phalaenopsis Party Poppers

PHALAENOPSIS

(*Ella Freed* × *stuartiana*) 'Harlequin'. The peloric markings on this hybrid are not a new innovation and cannot be easily reproduced by seed. It is merely a freak mutation which has occurred and is not as uncommon as in other genera.

PHALAENOPSIS PARTY POPPERS

(*Party Dress* × *lindenii*) 'Starlight Express'. New novelty hybrids are becoming more evident of late. In a novelty cross one parent invariably tends to be a species, while the other is sometimes a standard hybrid as in this case. These hybrids have such charm, with the plant and flowers perfectly balanced; this type of breeding is an ideal compliment to the larger standard Phalaenopsis.

PHALAENOPSIS GLYNDA FRIEDRICH

prominently features four species; namely, *P. violacea*, *P. mariae*, *P. amboinensis* and *P. sumatrana*. This hybrid must surely rate as being very close to the ultimate solid red Phalaenopsis hybrid.

Phaelaenopsis Glynda Friedrich

GLOSSARY

Alba/albino — Congenital absence of red pigments; such flowers are often white or yellow.

Aneuploid — The condition of the *chromosome* at the time of *meiosis* whereby one or more are missing or added to the normal number.

Anther — The part of a flower's stamen that contains pollen.

Autoclave — Apparatus similar to a pressure cooker and used to sterilize by steam under pressure.

Auxin — Plant growth hormone.

Back-bulb — Usually an older *pseudobulb*, often without leaves.

Chromosome — Rod-like structures within the nucleus of cells which carry the hereditary characteristics or *genes*.

Clone — Genetically identical plants which are derived from one original specimen.

Concolour — Being of only one colour; usually refers to *Albino* types of whites or yellows.

Cultivar — An original plant or vegetative propagation thereof. Derived from the term 'cultivated variety'.

Cytokinins — Plant growth additive which stimulates cell division.

Deciduous — Relating to plants that seasonally shed their leaves.

Differentiate — The process of change.

Diploid — A cell or organism containing twice the *haploid* number of *chromosomes*.

Epiphyte — Any plant which grows upon or clings to another merely for support. These plants are not parasitic.

Epiphytic — Pertaining to *epiphyte*.

Gene — Part of the *chromosome* which controls the hereditary characteristics.

Genus — A botanical collection of species which show similar characteristics. (Plural: genera.)

Grex — A collection or group of plants which are the progeny of a given cross.

Habitat — The natural origin of a plant.

Haploid — A cell containing only one representative from each pair of *chromosomes* found in a normal *diploid* cell.

Hybrid — The offspring derived from the crossing of two parents of different species or varieties.

Inflorescence — The arrangement of flowers sharing a common stalk.

Intergeneric — A hybrid derived from one or more genera (see *genus*).

Keiki — Hawaiian term relating to an offshoot from a plant.

Labellum — Lip, especially pertaining to an orchid.

Leaching — The process whereby excess mineral salts and soil nutrients are washed out or removed through watering.

Lithophyte — A plant which is usually found growing on rocks.

Lithophytic — Pertaining to *lithophyte*.

Mericlone — A plant produced by *meristem* or tissue culture.

Meristem — Vegetative propagation of plants, whereby tissue is taken from a plant in order to multiply genetically identical plants.

Monopodial — Term used to describe the group of plants in which the main axis of the stem continues to grow from the terminal bud.

Mycorrhiza — The intimate association between a specific fungus and the orchid seed; this is required for the seed to successfully germinate.

Node — Joint or knot on a stem.

Peloric — An abnormal formation, in which one or more parts of a flower simulate another part.

Pendulous — Hanging downwards.

Picot — Picottee – dark-edged petals or segments.

PLB — Protocorm Like Body – small mass of plant tissue similar to that of a *protocorm*.

Pollinia — Pollen – microspores or granules found in the *anthers*; male gametes.

Protocorm — Globular mass of plant tissue formed in the early stages of plant development.

Pseudobulb — Thickened, bulblike bases of certain orchids which are produced above ground.

Replated — The process of transplanting from flask to flask.

Species — A population of plants having one or more common characteristics which separate them from other such groups.

Spike — *Inflorescence* or flower stem.

Sympodial — Term used to describe the group of plants which have axial growth followed by lateral shoots or rhizomes.

Terrestrial — Soil loving plants.

Tetraploid — A cell or organism containing four times the *haploid* number of *chromosomes*.

Triploid — A cell or organism containing three times the *haploid* number of *chromosomes*; usually found to be sterile.

Vinicolour — Of wine red coloration.

Xanthotic — Pertaining to *albinism*.

INDEX

Acknowledgements

The authors wish to thank Joyce Stewart, Tessa Hedge, the Cymbidium Society of America, the Eric Young Orchid Foundation and Mile Thomas for assistance with photographs; Fiona Bilton for providing the line drawings; and Cathy Bilton, Veronica Pescod, Mike Gibson (and computer) and Sally Harper for their assistance.

Photographs on page 20 (centre) and page 35 (bottom) by Joyce Stewart; all others provided by Mike Tibbs/ McBeans Slide Library.